BRING-TO-LIFE
BOOK OF MORMON STORIES

BRING-TO-LIFE
BOOK OF MORMON STORIES
A Reference Guide for Speakers, Teachers, Students, and Parents

DAVID S. TAYLOR

BRING-TO-LIFE BOOK OF MORMON STORIES
A Reference Guide for Speakers, Teachers, Students, and Parents

The author may be contacted through his website at www.BookofMormonStories.net

Scripture taken from the King James Version of the Bible.

iUniverse books may be ordered through booksellers or by contacting:

iUniverse
1663 Liberty Drive
Bloomington, IN 47403
www.iuniverse.com
1-800-Authors (1-800-288-4677)

ISBN: 978-1-4917-7886-9 (sc)
ISBN: 978-1-4917-7887-6 (e)

Library of Congress Control Number: 2015915939

Print information available on the last page.

iUniverse rev. date: 10/14/2015

TABLE OF CONTENTS

PREFACE

Have you ever, as I have, been in a Sunday School class when the teacher asks, "Who could summarize the scripture story of XYZ for us?" Then there is a long pause, and you wish you had the courage to raise your hand, but you are not sure enough of the story details. Finally, a class member volunteers, but you think some important parts get left out.

The Book of Mormon is full of good stories. I saw a need to be prepared quickly to share them adequately in a class setting. I felt prompted and compelled to create a compilation of simple *Book of Mormon* story outlines that could be referenced on the spot to refresh one's memory about the important details of these glorious stories. I could see how such a collection would be a valuable aid, not only to students, but to teachers in classes, to parents in family home evenings, and to speakers in preparing talks, whether monthly as high councilmen or only occasionally as lay members.

Writing *Bring-to-Life Book of Mormon Stories* was a big project, a labor of love. Indeed, as I outlined the stories and analyzed the gospel principles taught therein, my love and understanding of this marvelous book of scripture increased greatly. It took me more than seven years to complete the *Reference Guide*. I did it a little at a time, line upon line. It was during a busy time in my life. I was working full-time as an engineer and scientist in the rocket business, serving as a leader in the Boy Scouts of America, raising a family of four children with my wife, and continually remodeling our house. Much of the writing was done on my lunch hours in blocks of ten to fifteen minutes. The typing had to be done at home, after work, over a period of about a year.

Don't get me wrong; I'm not one to shy away from big projects. It seems that I have always had one or two in the works. Just before starting on this one, I finished outlining the entire *Old Testament*, chapter by chapter, for my own personal use. Concurrently I published a guitar method book. You might think it strange for an engineer to be involved with teaching guitar. On the contrary, mathematics and logic have a great deal in common with music. My favorite classical composer is Alexander Borodin, who was a mathematician by trade. After earning my MBA degree, I organized and ran a retail music shop where I taught guitar and banjo lessons. My *E-Z Christmas Songs for Five-String Banjo* was published by Mel Bay during that time.

Unfortunately, my music business could not adequately support my growing family. I had to fall back on my BS degree in Chemical Engineering and enter the aerospace industry. In college, my professors told me I was strong in technical writing. Company training and experience built upon those skills. In my twenty-seven-year career, I was heavily involved in technical writing, mostly of rocket manufacturing instructions.

My writing approach is based on my training and experience as an engineer in reporting scientific research: observation, analysis, logical presentation, conciseness, and simplicity. These principles and skills apply across the board. In fact, they have become a way of life for me in both written and oral communications. In addition, my experience in teaching music on the side and in teaching teachers in my Church calling came into play. It was refreshing and uplifting to add a strong spiritual dimension to my technical approach as I compiled *Bring-to-Life Book of Mormon Stories*.

Composing the *Tips on Telling Stories from the Scriptures* for the first chapter reflected the quintessence of my style. For a teaching example of story-telling, I chose the encounter between Nathan and

David from the *Old Testament* for two reasons: 1) after all my years of studying the scriptures, it appeared that this was the best way to demonstrate story-telling, and 2) I felt strongly inspired in that direction. In the chapter, I applied all the elements of my writing skills to form a logical buildup, while maintaining the greatest respect for the dealings of God with men.

The Holy Bible has great stories, but there is something special about *The Book of Mormon*. It was written for our day. Moroni, as he finished the record of his father, Mormon, wrote to us, "Behold, I speak unto you as if ye were present ..." (Mormon 8:35). *Bring-to-Life Book of Mormon Stories* continue to inspire and motivate me as I study and share them. It is a dream come true to see this *Reference Guide* in print, after all these years, so that others may benefit by it.

ACKNOWLEDGMENTS

The author would like to thank the following good friends for their assistance in bringing forth this book:

David Hunsaker for teaching me how to handle a huge writing project by regularly and persistently setting aside time to digest the whole, a small bite at a time, until it is finally finished.

Jonathan Turner for the cover design. Heather Turner for editing.

Dan Bingham for publishing encouragement. Tracy Bingham for editing.

Susan Butler for her replicas of the gold plates and the Liahona pictured on the covers.

Rory and Michelle Weaver for great word-smithing suggestions and editing during the final stages of submission to the publisher.

My wife, Kathleen Taylor, for perspective and years of support.

INTRODUCTION

How to Get the Most Out of this *Reference Guide*

The Book of Mormon contains wonderful stories that can be used to learn and teach gospel principles. This *Reference Guide* is designed to help you select and review stories quickly, study them, and learn to bring them to life by telling them in your own words. Be sure to look at *Tips on Telling Stories from the Scriptures* in the first chapter to improve your story-telling effectiveness.

Bring-to-Life Book of Mormon Stories can be beneficial in many situations. This *Reference Guide* can help when:

* You have a speaking assignment and need a good scriptural story to liven up your talk while reinforcing your gospel subject.
* You are teaching a class and would like to use an example from *The Book of Mormon* to emphasize a point in your lesson.
* You are a student and would like to follow along with *The Book of Mormon* story being taught in class and want to be able to answer questions about it.
* You are a parent and want to teach a gospel principle to your child in family home evening or in a personal interview.

Choose the story that fits your circumstances by looking over the Table of Contents or one of the two indices in the back of the book. Turn to your chosen story and you will see in a simple format:

a) The title of the story,
b) The scriptural references (just those verses that apply to the story),
c) A brief background and outline of the story, and
d) Gospel principles that can easily be taught by the story.

For example, suppose you wanted to stress, in a talk or a lesson, the importance of having a good attitude. You would look in the *Index of Gospel Principles* under "A" for attitude. There you would be referred to several stories. Say you chose Story 10, Nephi Breaks His Bow. You would turn to it and read a brief summary of the story and how it applies to attitude. The next step would be to read the referenced verses in *The Book of Mormon* to become familiar enough with the story to tell it. Then you could apply the *Tips on Telling Stories from the Scriptures* as you prepare your presentation and bring your story to life with confidence.

Alternatively, to select your story, you could consult the *Index of People, Places, Things, and Events*. For instance, this second index would be useful if you were searching for a story about a certain:

- Person, such as Abinadi,
- Place, such as the land of Jershon,
- Thing, such as a temple, or
- Event, such as a baptism.

You may also find it enjoyable to read this book straight through, for your individual or family study. Thus, you can allow all of these inspiring *Bring-to-Life Book of Mormon Stories* to come to life along with the gospel principles that they teach.

May you find this *Reference Guide* useful and uplifting. And, may you feel the Spirit of the Lord as you put *Bring-to-Life Book of Mormon Stories* to good use.

TIPS ON TELLING STORIES
FROM THE SCRIPTURES

Anyone can tell a story. We do it all the time in our every-day conversations. Here are some tips that can help you be more effective in telling scriptural stories that live and teach.

1. **Seek the Spirit.** "Ask, and it shall be given unto you; seek, and ye shall find; knock, and it shall be opened unto you" (3 Nephi 14:7).

"And the Spirit shall be given unto you by the prayer of faith; and if ye receive not the Spirit ye shall not teach" (*D&C* 42:14). (Note: *D&C* is the abbreviation that will be used for *The Doctrine and Covenants of the Church of Jesus Christ of Latter-day Saints.*)

2. **Consider your audience.** What is the level of understanding, the maturity of those who will hear your story? Plan to give your audience the background that they need so that they can stay with you as the story is told. Use a slant to the story that will hold their interest.

"He that receiveth the word by the Spirit of truth receiveth it as it is preached by the Spirit of truth. Wherefore, he that preacheth and he that receiveth, understand one another, and both are edified and rejoice together" (*D&C* 50:21-22).

3. **Make your point.** Telling a story for the sake of story-telling is pointless. Put purpose into your story. In the purpose lies the power. Think of the way the Savior told parables and taught with them.

Let the way you tell the story emphasize the point you want to make. You may choose to read certain scriptural verses or parts of verses for emphasis. An occasional aside by the story-teller is very effective. A little humor can help, if appropriate.

Don't get carried away with giving too many details. Use only those that support your point and provide continuity to the story.

Ask a question for the listeners to ponder, such as, "How would you feel?" or "What would you think?" Then be sure to pause to allow them a moment to consider the question.

4. **Know your story.** Read the scriptural references over until you are familiar with the facts. Let your subconscious mind work for you: prepare in advance, ponder, and pray. Inspiration will be the result.

"Treasure up in your minds continually the words of life, and it shall be given you in the very hour that portion that shall be meted unto every man" (*D&C* 84:85).

5. **Build from the bottom.** Like a house, a story should be built in order, from the foundation up. Choose a starting point to match your audience. Give the necessary background. Then build your story, filling in the framework and the details as you go.

Remember that the roof comes later. Use suspense and then climax to finish off your story and drive your point home.

6. **Practice the telling.** Practice telling the story in your own words. Remember to include all the key points. Jot down the notes you need to guide you.

Use delivery techniques that will add to the power of the story, such as: voice inflections, pauses, facial expressions, and hand gestures.

"If ye are prepared ye shall not fear" (*D&C* 38:30).

<u>Examples:</u>

A great example of a well told story that forcefully brought home a point is that of Nathan telling David the parable of the ewe lamb. The story is found in 2 Samuel 11:1-27 and 12:1-14. (Note: All quotations from *The Holy Bible* will be taken from the King James Version.)

David was king over all Israel at the time. The Lord had delivered David out of the hands of Saul and had given him Saul's house and his wives. David possessed all that a man could desire. And, if that had not been enough, the Lord would have given him more.

At a time when David should have gone to battle with his servants, he tarried in Jerusalem. Unable to sleep, he walked upon his roof and saw the beautiful Bath-sheba washing herself. He was filled with unquenchable desire, which drove him to lie with her.

When he found out that she was with child, he tried to cover his sin by bringing her husband, Uriah, back from the front lines to be with his wife. But Uriah was too loyal to accept such luxuries while his fellow soldiers camped in tents.

David then compounded his sin by sending Uriah back to battle carrying orders for his own death. Joab, obedient to the King, assigned Uriah to a position where he was killed in battle.

After Bath-sheba's mourning for her husband was past, David took her to wife, and she bore his son. "But the thing that David had done displeased the Lord" (2 Samuel 11:27).

Nathan, the prophet, was in tune with the Spirit. He was prompted to go to David to tell him of the Lord's displeasure. He may well have pondered, prepared, and practiced his approach with the King as he traveled to the palace. He knew his audience: the King was a man of justice and had a great sense of fairness. By the time Nathan arrived, he was ready: the Lord would give him the words.

Nathan came unto David and told the story. He knew it well. It was simple and to the point. There was no hesitation, no faltering. There were no unnecessary details.

"There were two men in one city; the one rich, and the other poor.

"The rich man had exceeding many flocks and herds:

"But the poor man had nothing, save one little ewe lamb, which he had bought and nourished up: and it grew up together with him, and with his children; it did eat of his own meat, and drank of his own cup, and lay in his bosom, and was unto him as a daughter." (See 2 Samuel 12:1-3.)

Nathan had David's interest. You see, David had grown up as a shepherd. He had risked his life to save his sheep from a bear and a lion. You can almost feel the tension in the air as Nathan builds the suspense of the drama.

"And there came a traveler unto the rich man, and he spared to take of his own flock and of his own herd, to dress for the wayfaring man that was come unto him; but took the poor man's lamb, and dressed it for the man that was come to him" (2 Samuel 12:4).

Here, most certainly, Nathan paused.

The King was enraged! He flew into anger. Such injustice! "As the Lord liveth, the man that hath done this thing shall surely die," David exclaimed. (See 2 Samuel 12:5.)

Another pause and Nathan was ready to unleash the climax of his story, ready to drive home his point.

"And Nathan said to David, 'Thou art the man'" (2 Samuel 12:7).

Can you imagine how David felt? Wham! He had been hit right between the eyes. Convicted of his guilt, he saw the meaning of the parable. He could do nothing more than say, "I have sinned against the Lord" (2 Samuel 12:13).

Nathan had done a masterful job of telling his story.

* * *

In recounting the story of Nathan telling his parable to David, the author has attempted to apply his own tips as a second example. If you compare the way the author told his story to the scriptural reference in 2 Samuel 11:1-27 and 12:1-14, you will see what he did.

The key points were carefully chosen. Some details of the scripture were left out because they did not help to teach story-telling. Other details were rearranged so that the story could be built in order from the bottom up. Notice the background that was given to bring you up to the starting point of the story. Several verses were directly quoted for effect. In between quotations, the asides gave continuity and kept the focus on the lesson to be taught. Other parts of the story were told in the author's own words.

Questions were used to bring the reader into the drama. Pauses were built in with short paragraphs and sentences. The author sought the Spirit in writing these tips and relating this story of Nathan and David. Hopefully, you received by the Spirit. He considered his audience who, possibly, may have had limited experience telling scriptural stories.

Thus, you have this example within an example, two demonstrations of story-telling, one by Nathan and one by the author.

* * *

STORY 1

LEHI PREACHES IN JERUSALEM

Reference: 1 Nephi 1:4-15 and 18-20

Background: *Lehi lived with his family in Jerusalem shortly before the Babylonian captivity of Judah. His son, Nephi, made a record of proceedings in his days, starting with the experiences of his father. Lehi was one of the prophets who warned the people of the impending destruction of Jerusalem.*

Story Outline: Lehi prays for his people and sees visions of a pillar of fire, of God on His throne, of Christ descending with twelve apostles following Him, and of a book. The book tells of the abominations and destruction of Jerusalem, the coming of the Messiah, and the redemption of the world. Lehi praises God and rejoices at His mercy for sparing those who come unto Him. He goes amongst the people and prophesies of the things he has seen and heard. The Jews are angry with Lehi. They mock him and seek to take his life.

Gospel Principles:

1. **Mercy.**
   - God warns people through His prophets so that they can repent and be saved. (See v. 4.)
   - God will deliver those who come unto Him. (See v. 14.)

- Nephi will show that God was merciful in delivering Lehi's family. (See v. 20.)
- Notwithstanding the predicted destruction of Jerusalem, Lehi and Nephi were impressed with God's mercy.

2. **Persecution.** The Jews were angry with Lehi and the other prophets because they testified of the wickedness of the people. (See v. 20.)

3. **Prayer.** Lehi prayed with all his heart for his people. (See v. 5.)

4. **Prophecy.** The destruction of Jerusalem and Babylonian captivity were prophesied shortly before they actually occurred. (See v. 13.)

5. **Prophets.** God reveals His will and warns His people through prophets. (See v. 4.)

6. **Revelation.** Lehi's prayer for his people was answered with a revelation from God. (See v. 6.)

* * *

STORY 2

LEHI TAKES HIS FAMILY INTO THE WILDERNESS

Reference: 1 Nephi 2:1-7

Background: *Lehi, having lived in Jerusalem all his days, and having been warned of God, prophesied of the impending destruction of the city. The Jews rejected his testimony and sought to take his life. His son, Nephi, kept a record of his father's proceedings. (See Story 1.)*

Story Outline: The Lord speaks to Lehi in a dream, commends him for his faithfulness, warns him that the people seek his life, and commands him to take his family out of Jerusalem into the wilderness. His family consists of his wife, Sariah, and his four sons, Laman, Lemuel, Sam, and Nephi.

Lehi obeys. He leaves his house, land, and precious things, taking only his family, provisions, and tents into the borders by the Red Sea. After three days journey, he sets up camp, builds an altar, and gives thanks to God.

Gospel Principles:

1. **Divine guidance.** Lehi's experience identifies two areas in which we may expect God's help in our lives:

a) If we live in tune with the Spirit we may be warned of dangers to avoid.

b) When and where to move our families is a big enough decision to warrant seeking the Lord's direction.

2. **Gratitude**. Though he had to leave behind nearly all of his worldly possessions, Lehi still realized that the Lord had blessed him by saving him and his family. He remembered to build an altar and give thanks. (See v. 7.)

3. **Obedience.**
    * Lehi was faithful in declaring to the people the things God commanded of him. (See v. 1)
    * Lehi was obedient to the word of the Lord to take his family out of Jerusalem. (See v. 2-4.)

4. **Revelation.** Lehi was told in a dream that he was blessed for his faithfulness, that the people sought his life, and that he should take his family and depart into the wilderness. (See v. 1-2.)

5. **Sacrifice.** Lehi left behind his worldly possessions, house, land, gold, silver, and precious things, to follow the Lord's commandment to go into the wilderness. How much are we willing to give up to serve the Lord?

* * *

STORY 3

LAMAN AND LEMUEL MURMUR AGAINST THEIR FATHER

Reference: 1 Nephi 2:6-24

Background: *Lehi was warned in a dream to leave Jerusalem and take his family, consisting of his wife and four sons, into the wilderness. He obeyed, leaving behind all worldly possessions but tents and provisions. This was according to the record of Nephi. (See Story 2.)*

Story Outline: Laman and Lemuel, the two oldest sons of Lehi, murmur against their father in many things. They know not the dealings of God and do not believe Jerusalem can be destroyed as Lehi prophesied. Laman and Lemuel blame their trip into the wilderness on foolish imaginations of their father. Inspired by the Spirit, Lehi instructs his sons with power, comparing Laman to a river and Lemuel to a valley.

Nephi, Lehi's youngest son, prays and receives a testimony of his father's words. Therefore, he does not rebel like his older brothers. Instead, he converts his brother, Sam, and tries to reason with Laman and Lemuel, who will not hearken. Nephi prays for his brethren and is told by the Lord that keeping the commandments brings blessing while rebellion brings cursing.

Gospel Principles:

1. **Attitude.** Laman and Lemuel were stiffnecked, critical, and doubting. They murmured against their father and were unwilling to listen to their younger brother. On the other hand, Nephi and Sam were soft-hearted, teachable, and believing. (Compare v. 11-13 with v. 16-18.)

2. **Diligence.** Nephi was commended for his diligence in seeking after the Lord. (See v. 16 and 19.)

3. **Faith.** The older brothers were unbelieving even as the Jews at Jerusalem. Yet, Nephi demonstrated his faith by calling upon the Lord to know of the things of God. (Compare v. 13 and 18 with v. 16 and 19.)

4. **Holy Ghost.** The power of the Holy Ghost was manifest in Lehi as he spoke to his murmuring sons until their frames shook before him. (See v. 14.)

5. **Honoring parents.** Laman and Lemuel murmured against their father and doubted his motives. Nephi believed his father and supported him by being obedient and trying to convince his brothers to do likewise. (Compare v. 11-12 with v. 16.)

6. **Humility.** Nephi sought the Lord with lowliness of heart. (See v. 19.)

7. **Parenthood.** Lehi counseled his sons with love. He yearned that they would always seek after righteousness and be firm and steadfast. Lehi named a river and a valley after Laman and Lemuel, respectively, and compared the strengths of the geologic features to them. When moved upon by the Spirit, Lehi spoke to the rebellious ones with power to bring them to obedience. (See v. 8-10 and 14.)

8. **Prayer.**
   - Nephi cried unto the Lord because he had a desire to know the mysteries of God. Because of his faith, diligence, and humility, he received his answer. (See v. 16 and 19.)
   - Nephi prayed for his stubborn brothers. (See v. 18.) Do we pray regularly for our family members who have hardened their hearts?

9. **Remembrance.** When things are running smoothly, how easily we forget that our blessings come from God. The Lord sends scourges to humble us and bring us to remembrance. (See v. 24.)

10. **Revelation.**
    - Nephi's prayers were answered, his heart was softened, and he believed his father's words. (See v. 16-17.) Just like Nephi, we need to receive our own confirmation by the Spirit.
    - When Nephi prayed for his brothers, the Lord told him of things to come upon his seed and the seed of his brethren. (See v. 19 ff.)

11. **Reward for righteousness.** Those who keep the commandments will prosper. Nephi was promised a choice land and opportunity to be a ruler and a teacher over his older brothers. (See v. 20 and 22.)

12. **Reward for wickedness.** Rebels will be cut off from God's presence. They will receive cursing instead of blessing. (See v. 21 and 23.)

13. **Testimony.** Lehi had received divine guidance for his family from the Lord. He had a testimony. It was up to his sons to develop their own testimonies of his words. Laman and Lemuel hardened their hearts, murmured, and rebelled. Nephi had the desire to know for himself and sought the Lord in

diligence and humility. He shared his manifestation with his brother, Sam, who then gained a testimony. But Laman and Lemuel would not hearken to Nephi's words. (See v. 12-13 and 16-18.)

* * *

STORY 4

LEHI'S SONS OBTAIN
THE BRASS PLATES

Reference: 1 Nephi 3:1-31; 4:1-38; 5:20-22

Background: *Lehi and his family were living in tents in the wilderness after leaving Jerusalem. Lehi's older sons, Laman and Lemuel, murmured against their father, while the younger sons, Nephi and Sam, believed and supported Lehi. (See Story 3.)*

Story Outline: Lehi tells Nephi about his dream wherein the Lord commanded him to send his sons back to Jerusalem to obtain the brass plates from Laban. The plates contain records of the Jews and a genealogy of Lehi's forefathers. Nephi, unlike his murmuring older brothers, is faithful and willing to obey and go.

Nephi and his brothers return to Jerusalem. The lot falls on Laman to go talk to Laban about getting the plates. Laban is angry and thrusts Laman out as an accused robber. The brothers are discouraged and would give up, but Nephi is firm in accomplishing their mission. He suggests that they go to their father's land of inheritance to get their abandoned riches for use in persuading Laban. Nephi reminds his brothers of the importance of the records they were sent to obtain.

After gathering their gold, silver, and precious things, the four brothers go before Laban with an offer of exchange for the records. Laban seizes their property and sends his servants to kill them. They escape and hide in a cave. Laman and Lemuel are angry and smite Nephi and Sam with a rod. An angel intervenes, chastising the older brothers, and commanding them to go back again to Jerusalem where Laban will be delivered into their hands. Laman and Lemuel murmur and doubt the angel's words, for they fear Laban's might. Full of faith, Nephi knows that the Lord is mightier than Laban and his fifty men. Nephi persuades his murmuring brothers, against their protests, to follow him back to Jerusalem.

Lehi's sons approach Jerusalem by night. Leaving his brothers hidden without the city walls, Nephi proceeds to Laban's house alone, to act as led by the Spirit. He finds Laban drunken and fallen to the earth. Nephi draws Laban's sword and is constrained by the Spirit to kill him. He struggles within himself but finally is obedient to the voice of the Spirit and smites off Laban's head. After putting on the dead man's garments and armor, Nephi proceeds to the treasury to get the brass plates. He meets Laban's servant, Zoram, and poses as his master, conversing with him about the elders of the Jews whom Laban had visited that night. The disguised Nephi bids Zoram to carry the records and follow him to meet his brothers outside the city walls.

When Laman and his brothers see the two men approaching them, they think that Nephi is Laban and start to flee. Nephi calls after them and they stop. But now, Zoram fears and is ready to flee, so Nephi seizes and holds him. Nephi promises Zoram safety and freedom and convinces him to join with Lehi's family. The five men return with the records to the tent of Lehi in the wilderness.

Gospel Principles:

1. **Courage.** Nephi had the courage to go back up to Jerusalem after Laban had sought to kill him and his brothers. He even went into

the city alone at night. (See 1 Nephi 4:1-3 and 5.) Contrast the lack of courage displayed by Laman and Lemuel. (See 1 Nephi 3:31.)

2. **Diligence.** Nephi persisted until the commandment was accomplished. He went to Laban three times even though his brothers strove to stop him even unto smiting him with a rod.

3. **Divine guidance.** Faithful Nephi was "led by the Spirit, not knowing beforehand the things which (he) should do." (See 1 Nephi 4:6.) It is imperative that we rely on the Lord to guide us when we are on His errand. We are told, "It shall be given you … in the very moment, what ye shall say." (See *D&C* 100:5-6; 84:85.)

4. **Faith.**
   • Nephi was full of faith that they would succeed in their mission because he knew the Lord would prepare the way. (See 1 Nephi 3:7.)
   • Unlike his older brothers, Nephi trusted in the words of the angel. He knew the Lord would give them power even like unto Moses when the Israelites were pursued by Pharaoh. (Compare 1 Nephi 4:1-3 with 1 Nephi 3:31.)

5. **Holy Ghost.** Nephi relied upon the Spirit to guide him as he went back to the house of Laban. The prompting from the Holy Ghost to slay Laban was strong. Nephi heard a voice and was brought to remember previous counsel. (See 1 Nephi 4:5-6 and 10-18.)

6. **Obedience.** Nephi was willing to go right out and do what he was commanded to do. (See 1 Nephi 3:7 and 15; 4:1.) Due largely to Nephi's faithfulness in obeying the Lord, the brothers accomplished their mission to get the plates. (See 1 Nephi 5:20-21.)

7. **Records.** In this story, the importance of the brass plates is emphasized by the Lord, by Lehi, and by Nephi. The records

were of great worth to the family for preserving their language, their genealogy, the words of the prophets, and the laws and commandments of God. The value of Laban's wicked life was far outweighed by the need of Lehi's family for keeping their posterity from perishing in unbelief. (See 1 Nephi 3:3-4 and 19-20; 4:13-17; 5:21-22.)

* * *

STORY 5

SARIAH DOUBTS AND COMPLAINS

<u>Reference</u>: 1 Nephi 5:1-9

<u>Background</u>: *While living in a tent in the wilderness, Lehi, in obedience to the Lord's command, sent his sons back to Jerusalem to obtain the brass plates, which contained a record of the Jews and Lehi's genealogy. After three difficult attempts, the brothers, led by Nephi, were successful in getting the plates from Laban. (See Story 4.)*

<u>Story Outline</u>: While Nephi and his brothers are gone on their mission to obtain the brass plates, their mother, Sariah, worries that they have perished. She complains against her husband, Lehi, calling him a visionary man for leading the family into the wilderness. Lehi admits that he is a visionary man and comforts his wife by expressing his faith that the Lord will deliver their sons and bring them back safely.

When the sons return to Lehi's tent with the plates, Lehi and Sariah rejoice greatly. Their joy is full. Sariah is comforted and says that she now knows that her husband was commanded by the Lord to bring the family out of Jerusalem. She also now knows surely that her sons were given power and protection from the Lord in accomplishing their purpose. The family gives thanks and offers sacrifice unto the Lord.

Gospel Principles:

1. **Attitude.** Sariah's complaint against her husband that he was a visionary man who had led the family out of the land of their inheritance was the same that she had heard from her older sons. (Compare v. 2 with Story 3.) A bad attitude can be contagious.

2. **Faith.** Lehi maintained his faith in the face of complaints by his older sons and his wife. (See Story 3 and v. 4-5 in this story.) Sometimes our faith is tested by our loved ones who do not believe.

3. **Gratitude.** Sariah realized that her sons were delivered by the Lord. She and her husband were filled with joy at the return of their sons. The family remembered to give thanks to the Lord. (See v. 9.)

4. **Joy.** Lehi and Sariah were filled with joy to see their sons again. (See v. 1 and 9.) True joy comes from being with our families.

5. **Love.**
    *   The love the parents had for their sons was evident in their joy at the safe return of their sons. (See v. 1 and 9.)
    *   Lehi showed his love for his wife by comforting her when she complained against him rather than complaining back. (See v. 3-6.)

6. **Parenthood.** Both mother and father showed their concern and love for their sons. (See v. 1-2.) Parents naturally worry about their children when they don't return home on time.

7. **Patience.** Lehi was an example of patience in waiting for his sons to return and in dealing with his wife's complaints. (See v. 4-6.)

8. **Testimony.** Lehi bore his testimony to his wife to comfort her and lift her up. (See v. 4-5.) We all become discouraged at times. Your testimony can be a tool for cheering someone up.

* * *

STORY 6

LEHI'S SONS BRING ISHMAEL'S FAMILY INTO THE WILDERNESS

Reference: 1 Nephi 7:1-22

Background: *Lehi and his family, having fled Jerusalem, were living in tents in the wilderness. His sons had returned from a journey back to Jerusalem where they had obtained the brass plates containing a record of the Jews. (See Stories 4 and 5.) After reading the plates, Lehi, inspired by the Spirit, prophesied concerning his seed.*

Story Outline: After Lehi finishes prophesying, the Lord speaks to him. Lehi is told to send his sons back to Jerusalem again, this time to bring Ishmael and his family into the wilderness so that his sons can marry Ishmael's daughters and raise families.

Nephi and his brothers return to Jerusalem and proceed to Ishmael's house. They find favor with Ishmael, and by speaking the words of the Lord convince him and his family to journey with them.

On the group's way to Lehi's tent in the wilderness, Laman and Lemuel lead a rebellion and want to return to Jerusalem. Nephi tries to persuade them to be faithful, reminding them of the Lord's dealings with them. His brothers are angry at his words. They seize Nephi and bind him with cords to leave him to die.

Nephi prays to the Lord to be delivered and his bands are loosed. He speaks to his brothers again. Though Laman and Lemuel are angry at first, their hearts are softened by the pleading of members of Ishmael's family. The rebellious ones repent and ask Nephi's forgiveness, which he freely grants. After prayers to God for forgiveness, they all finish their journey to Lehi's tent.

Gospel Principles:

1. **Faith.** Nephi had the faith that his bands could be broken through the power of the Lord. And they were loosed. (See v. 17-18.)

2. **Forgiveness.** Nephi frankly forgave his brethren even though they sought to take away his life. (See v. 20-21.)

3. **Gratitude.** Lehi remembered to give thanks and offer sacrifice unto the Lord after his sons returned successful. (See v. 22.)

4. **Holy Ghost.** The Spirit of the Lord spoke through Nephi to warn the rebellious group that they would perish if they returned to Jerusalem. (See v. 15.) The Holy Ghost may prompt us to warn us of danger. If we heed the still small voice, we will be safe.

5. **Prayer.**
    *   When Nephi was in danger of losing his life, he knew where to turn. His prayer for deliverance was answered immediately and his bands were loosed. (See v. 16-18.)
    *   Prayer to ask the Lord for forgiveness was an important part of the repentance by those who rebelled and bound Nephi. (See v. 21.)

6. **Repentance.** Laman, Lemuel, and the others recognized their sin, were sorrowful and asked Nephi and the Lord for forgiveness. (See v. 20-21.)

7. **Revelation.** Lehi was given inspiration to prophesy concerning
   his seed. He was commanded to send his sons to bring Ishmael's
   family with them. (See v. 1-2.) The Lord knew what was for the
   best good of Lehi and his family and revealed it to the family head.

* * *

STORY 7

LEHI HAS A DREAM OF THE TREE AND THE ROD OF IRON

Reference: 1 Nephi 8:2-38; 11:1-36; 12:1-23; 15:1-11 and 21-36

Background: *Lehi and his family, living in tents in the wilderness, were joined by Ishmael and his family whom Lehi's sons had persuaded to come out of Jerusalem with them. (See Story 6.)*

Story Outline: Lehi speaks to his family and tells them of a dream he dreamed, which caused him to rejoice for Nephi and Sam and to fear for Laman and Lemuel. In his dream Lehi is led through a dark and dreary waste to a large and spacious field. He sees a tree with fruit that is exceedingly white and desirable to make one happy. Lehi eats of the fruit and discovers that it is most sweet and desirable above all other fruit; he is filled with joy from it. Desiring to share the fruit with his family, Lehi looks around for them. He sees Sariah, Nephi, and Sam at the head of a river, which runs near the tree. They respond to his call to come and partake of the fruit. But Laman and Lemuel refuse to come and partake.

Lehi sees a rod of iron, with a strait and narrow path beside it, leading along the bank of the river to the tree. Numerous people are trying to obtain the path to the tree. A mist of darkness causes some of the people who have started on the path to lose their way and wander off. Others hold to the rod, reach the tree, partake of the fruit, then become ashamed because they are scoffed at by the finely dressed people in a great building across the river. Some people, including Nephi, press forward holding to the rod until they obtain the fruit and do not heed those who scorn. Many seek their way toward the spacious building to join those who are mocking and pointing their fingers at those eating the fruit. Still others are drowned in the river or are lost on strange roads.

Lehi is concerned about Laman and Lemuel because of the dream, and he exhorts them to keep the commandments.

Nephi desires to see the things his father saw and has the faith to do so. He is caught away by the Spirit and is shown Lehi's dream with the interpretation in conjunction with a vision of the life of the Son of God. Nephi sees the Virgin Mary, the infant Jesus, John the Baptist baptizing the Lamb of God, Christ's ministry, the twelve apostles, and the crucifixion. Nephi is shown the land of promise for his seed, the visit of the resurrected Savior, the twelve Nephite disciples, the three generations of peace, and the final battles and destruction of his people.

After the vision, Nephi returns to the tent of his father. He finds his brothers disputing with one another over the words their father had spoken to them. After reproving them for the hardness of their hearts in not inquiring of the Lord, Nephi answers their questions about Lehi's dream.

In Lehi's dream:

    a) The tree represents the tree of life or the love of God. (See 1 Nephi 11:21-23 and 25; 15:21-22; John 3:16.)

    b) The rod of iron is the word of God. (See 1 Nephi 11:25; 15:23-24.) (Note that in *The Bible,* John refers to Christ as the Word in John 1:1-2 and 1 John 5:7.)

    c) The river of water represents filthiness or the depths of hell. (See 1 Nephi 12:16 and 18; 15:26-30.)

d) The spacious building represents the world and the wisdom, vain imaginations, and pride thereof. (See 1 Nephi 11:35-36; 12:18.)

e) The mists of darkness are the temptations of the Devil. (See 1 Nephi 12:17.)

Gospel Principles:

1. **Atonement.** Nephi was shown that the Lamb of God would be slain for the sins of the world. (See 1 Nephi 11:32-33.)

2. **Enduring.** To obtain our eternal reward we must always press forward, holding tightly to the word of God. By so doing we can ignore the scoffs and scorns of the world and overcome the temptations of the adversary. (See 1 Nephi 8:30 and 33; 15:24.)

3. **Faith.** Nephi believed that the Lord could make known to him the things that his father had seen. Because he believed the words of his father and believed in the Son of God, the Spirit showed him the things he desired to see. (See 1 Nephi 11:1 and 4-6.)

4. **Family.** When Lehi discovered that the fruit of the tree of life filled him with great joy, he wanted to share it with his family. He was concerned that all of his family members were not willing to come partake of the fruit. (See 1 Nephi 8:3-4 and 12-18.)

5. **Jesus Christ.** This vision contains much symbolism representing the Savior, who is the Life of the World, the Living Water, the Love of God, and the Word. (See 1 Nephi 11:21-26; John 1:1-2; 3:16; 1 John 5:7.)

6. **Joy.** The fruit of the tree of life, or the love of God, is the most sweet and most desirable above all for obtaining exceeding great joy. (See 1 Nephi 8:10-12; 11:22-23.)

7. **Love.** The love of God, represented by the tree of life, is the greatest of all the gifts of God. It is spread abroad in the hearts of

men and is the most desirable above all other things. (See 1 Nephi 11:21-23 and 25; 15:36.)

8. **Parenthood.** Lehi was concerned over some members of his family who would not come and partake of the fruit even though he beckoned and called to them. With love and tender feeling, he preached, prophesied, and exhorted Laman and Lemuel to keep God's commandments. (See 1 Nephi 8:3-4, 14-18 and 36-38.)

9. **Peer pressure.** It is as true now as it was then. Those of the world will scoff, scorn, make fun, mock, and point their fingers to make those who try to do right feel ashamed. (See 1 Nephi 8:24-28.)

10. **Pondering.** As Nephi sat pondering in his heart, the Spirit carried him away. (See 1 Nephi 11:1.)

11. **Power of God.** The miracles performed by the Savior during his earthly ministry are manifestations of his power. (See 1 Nephi 11:31.)

12. **Pride.** The people in the spacious building were lifted up in pride to the point of persecuting the humble followers of the word of God. Their manner of dress was very fine, and they imagined themselves to be better than other people. (See 1 Nephi 8:26-27 and 33; 12:18-19.)

13. **Revelation.** Lehi's dream or vision was given to benefit him and his family. Nephi exercised three key principles for obtaining revelation. He: 1) had the desire, 2) displayed the faith, and 3) pondered in his heart. (See 1 Nephi 8:2; 11:1.)

14. **Reward for righteousness.** The fruit of the tree of life is most sweet and most desirable to make one happy. The love of God, which the fruit represents, is the greatest of all the gifts of God and most joyous to the soul. Only those who press forward and

endure to the end will obtain the reward. (See 1 Nephi 8:10-12; 11:21-23; 15:36.)

15. **Reward for wickedness.** Those who fight against the twelve apostles will fall and be destroyed. The wicked will be separated from the tree of life and from the saints. They will be judged and, if found filthy, shall be cast off into that hell prepared for them. (See 1 Nephi 11:36; 15:26-29 and 33-36.)

16. **Seeking.** Because Nephi had the desire, inquired of the Lord in faith, and was receptive to the Spirit, he came to understand his father's teachings. On the other hand, his brothers hardened their hearts, did not keep the commandments, and did not ask the Lord. Therefore, Laman and Lemuel did not understand Lehi's words and disputed amongst themselves. (See 1 Nephi 11:1; 15:2-4 and 8-11.)

17. **Steadfastness.** To obtain the reward we must hold fast to the word of God, letting it guide us through the temptations and persecutions of life. (See 1 Nephi 8:30 and 33; 15:24.)

18. **Temptation.** The mists of darkness in Lehi's dream graphically represent the temptations, which blind us and make us lose our way along the path to eternal life. Many people wander, lost on the strange roads of the diversity of sins. (See 1 Nephi 8:23 and 32; 12:17 and19; 15:24.)

19. **Worldliness.** The world knows not of and is separated from the sacred fruit of the tree of life. Their focus is on spacious buildings, fine clothes, man's wisdom, vain imaginations, and ridiculing of the humble followers of the word of God. Multitudes seek the things of this world. However, worldliness is a false goal, which will not bring happiness but destruction. (See 1 Nephi 8:26-27, 31 and 33; 11:35-36.)

* * *

STORY 8

NEPHI KEEPS TWO SETS OF PLATES

Reference: 1 Nephi 9:1-6; 19:1-5; 2 Nephi 5:29-33; Words of Mormon 1:1-7; *D&C* 10:1, 6-34 and 38-45

Background: *Nephi kept a record of the proceedings in his days. He chronicled the experiences of his father, Lehi, who was warned by the Lord to leave the soon to be destroyed city of Jerusalem with this family. While dwelling in a tent in the valley of Lemuel in the wilderness, Lehi and Nephi beheld a dream of the tree and the rod of iron. (See Stories 1 through 7.)*

Story Outline: Nephi receives a commandment to keep a separate set of plates for recording the ministry of his people, the prophecies, and the more sacred things. The plates are to be distinct and different from the other plates, which contain a more full account of the history of the people, their kings, wars, contentions, and destructions. The commandment is for a wise and special purpose in the Lord, which Nephi does not understand. Nevertheless, Nephi trusts in the Lord, who knows all things from the beginning, and is obedient in making the second set of plates. On these separate, smaller plates he engraves the things that are pleasing unto God.

Nephi commands his people to keep the records and hand down the plates from generation to generation after he is gone.

Over nine hundred years later, while abridging the larger plates of Nephi, which contain the more part of the history, Mormon discovers the second set, the smaller plates of Nephi, containing the prophecies and revelations. The things recorded thereon are pleasing and choice unto him. For a wise purpose, which he does not understand either, Mormon, as directed by the Spirit, includes these small plates with the remainder of his record.

Still another fourteen hundred years or so later, Joseph Smith translates *The Book of Mormon* starting with Mormon's abridgement of the larger plates of Nephi. Joseph lets Martin Harris take 116 pages of the translated manuscript. The pages are lost into the hands of wicked men who are persuaded to carry out the Devil's cunning plan to destroy the work of God. They will alter the words of the lost manuscript and ask Joseph to translate them again. When the new translation does not agree with the altered manuscript, the wicked men will refute the work to get glory of the world.

The Lord commands Joseph Smith not to translate the same words again, rather to work from the smaller plates of Nephi, covering the same period. Thus, by the foreknowledge and power of the Lord, the Devil's plan is frustrated and the wicked men are confounded.

Gospel Principles:

1. **Faith.** Both Nephi and Mormon demonstrated their faith in the Lord by including the small plates with the records even though they did not know the full purpose for doing so. By their obedience, they showed their trust that the Lord knows all things. (See 1 Nephi 9:5-6; Words of Mormon 1:7.)

2. **Holy Ghost.** Through the whisperings of the Spirit of the Lord, Mormon knew to include the small plates with the rest of the records. (See Words of Mormon 1:7.) Do we listen to and obey the whisperings of the Holy Ghost?

3. **Journals.** The two types of plates kept by Nephi can guide us in our journal writing. (See 1 Nephi 9:3-4; 19:1-5.) Our secular

history may be interesting to our posterity, but let us not leave out the more sacred things of our lives, i.e., our testimonies and spiritual experiences.

4. **Obedience.** Without fully understanding the Lord's purpose, Nephi and Mormon trusted and obeyed the Lord concerning the extra set of plates. (See 1 Nephi 9:5-6; Words of Mormon 1:7.) Do we obey the commandments even when we may not be convinced in our minds of the purpose? Faith and obedience go hand in hand.

5. **Opposition.** The opposing, eternal forces of good and evil are seen to be at work in this story over a period of several centuries.

6. **Power of God.** God's wisdom is superior to Satan's. The Lord knows all things from the beginning to the end. He has power to bring to pass all his words. (See 1 Nephi 9:5-6; 19:3; Words of Mormon 1:7; *D&C* 10:43.)

7. **Records.** The second set of plates was necessary so that future generations would have instruction and knowledge of the more sacred things. The Lord and Satan, working in opposing directions, realized the importance of the work of bringing forth *The Book of Mormon*. (See 1 Nephi 9:3-4; 19:3 and 5; *D&C* 10:12, 14, 33 and 40-43.)

8. **Satan.** Satan works in direct opposition to the purposes of the Lord. He uses lies, flattery, deceit and promises of glory to try to destroy the souls of men and the work of God. (See *D&C* 10:10-29.)

9. **Teaching.** The scriptures are necessary for teaching the gospel and preserving our knowledge of the things of God. (See 1 Nephi 9:3 and 5; 2 Nephi 5:30-32.)

* * *

STORY 9

A COMPASS (LIAHONA) GUIDES LEHI'S FAMILY

Reference: 1 Nephi 16:6-17, 23 and 26-32; 18:11-13 and 21; Alma 37:38-46

Background: *Nephi wrote about the things that were said and done as his father's (Lehi's) family and the family of Ishmael (see Story 6) left Jerusalem and were dwelling in tents in the wilderness. Our record comes from a separate set of plates that Nephi was commanded to keep for recording the ministry of his people. (See Story 8.) Lehi's four sons and Zoram (see Story 4) took Ishmael's daughters to wife. (See 1 Nephi 16:7.)*

Story Outline: Lehi is commanded by the Lord to journey farther into the wilderness. In the morning at his tent door, he finds a brass ball of curious workmanship. One of the two spindles on the ball points the way for the families on their journey, keeping them in the more fertile parts of the wilderness where they can slay food.

Nephi discovers that the pointers and the writing on the ball work according to the faith, diligence, and heed that are given to them. A warning appears in writing on the ball when family members murmur against God because their bows are all broken. (See Story 10.)

Later, on the group's voyage across the sea, the ball or compass stops working when Nephi's brothers bind him. A great storm arises, and the rebels do not know where they should steer the ship. After the rebellious brothers let Nephi loose, the compass begins working again. Nephi prays and the storm subsides. (See Story 12.)

In the book of Alma, we read of Alma teaching his son, Helaman, about the Liahona (the brass ball or director) and how it worked to guide their fathers in the wilderness. He compares following the compass for temporal guidance to following the word of Christ for spiritual direction.

Gospel Principles:

1. **Diligence.** The compass worked according to the diligence that was shown it. As an example, Nephi was diligent in following the directions on the ball to find food. (See 1 Nephi 16:28-32; Alma 37:41-46.) So it is with us. If we diligently follow the direction we are given by the scriptures and our Church leaders, we will obtain the reward.

2. **Divine guidance.** When we receive the gift of the Holy Ghost, we are given our own internal compasses to guide us on our journeys through life. However, receiving guidance takes effort and practice: exercising faith, giving heed, and being diligent. If we regularly ignore the still small voice of our personal Liahonas, our messages from above will dwindle into silence. (See 1 Nephi 16:28; Alma 37:40 and 43.)

3. **Faith.** The Liahona worked for the travelers according to their faith in God that He would cause the spindles to point the way. (See 1 Nephi 16:28; Alma 37:40-41.) By faith marvelous works are brought to pass.

4. **Holy Ghost.** The gift of the Holy Ghost operates much like the Liahona. It is effective as we give faith, diligence, and heed to it. It

will lead us in the proper paths. If we do the things that are wrong, we lose its guidance. Through repentance we can again be worthy to receive direction. (See 1 Nephi 16:16; 18:12-13 and 21.)

5. **Obedience.** The compass was only as useful as the heed they gave unto it. (See 1 Nephi 16:28-32; Alma 37:41-46.) Similarly, only as we obey the word of Christ will we prosper and keep on the straight course to eternal life.

6. **Power of God.** The Lord often works by small means, simple commandments, to bring about his purposes. The human mind tends to look for magnificent, glorious miracles and overlook the plain solutions provided by the Lord. (See 1 Nephi 16:29; Alma 37:41.)

7. **Reward for righteousness.** As we have faith, repent, and give diligent heed to the words of Christ we will stay on course to our eternal reward. (See 1 Nephi 18:21; Alma 37:44-45.)

8. **Reward for wickedness.** Lehi's family suffered hardship on land and sea when they were disobedient. (See 1 Nephi 18:13; Alma 37:41-42.) Even so, our transgressions take us off course on our journey to the eternal promised land.

9. **Slothfulness.** When Lehi's family did not exercise their faith and diligence they did not progress. (See Alma 37:41-46.) Continual diligence in the routine obedience to God's commands in our everyday lives is requisite for obtaining the prize.

10. **Teaching.** Notice the masterful teaching technique of Alma as he exhorted his son to diligent obedience. He used the ancestral story of the Liahona as a type or shadow with an application to his son's present life. (See Alma 37:38-46.)

* * *

STORY 10

NEPHI BREAKS HIS BOW

Reference: 1 Nephi 16:15-32

Background: *Lehi's family, now united with the family of Ishmael by marriage, was traveling in the wilderness as directed by the curious ball (compass) provided by the Lord. (See Story 9.) They obtained food along the way by slaying beasts with their bows and arrows, stones, and slings.*

Story Outline: As Nephi goes forth to slay food, he breaks his bow of fine steel. Since his brothers' bows had lost their springs, the party is left without means of obtaining food. Laman and Lemuel are angry with their brother, Nephi. They, the sons of Ishmael, and even Lehi murmur because of their sufferings and afflictions in the wilderness.

Nephi exhorts his brethren not to complain against the Lord. He makes a bow out of wood and asks his father where he should go to obtain food. Lehi, humbled by Nephi's words, inquires of the Lord. The Lord chastens Lehi and tells him to look upon the ball where he sees a warning that causes him to tremble with fear.

Nephi follows the directions given upon the compass and is successful at slaying food at the top of the mountain. When he returns with the food, his family is joyful, humble, and grateful.

<u>Gospel Principles:</u>

1. **Attitude.** Laman and Lemuel were angry at Nephi when he broke his bow. Others in the group joined in their murmuring and complaining about their afflictions. On the other hand, Nephi kept a proper attitude. Rather than complaining, he set to work to solve the problem by making a bow of wood. (Compare v. 18-20 with v. 21-23.)

2. **Diligence.** Nephi did not give up even under exceedingly difficult conditions. He exhorted the others not to complain against God. (See v. 21-23.)

3. **Discouragement.** When things go wrong, it is easy to become discouraged even unto complaining against the Lord.

4. **Faith.** Nephi retained his faith through this trial. He knew that his father could find out from the Lord where to go to obtain food. (See v. 23.)

5. **Honoring parents.** Even though Lehi was amongst the murmurers, Nephi still followed the patriarchal order by asking his father where to go to find food. (See v. 23.)

6. **Humility.** Lehi's family humbled themselves and acknowledged the Lord's hand because of Nephi's admonishing and also when they saw that food was provided for them. (See v. 24 and 32.)

7. **Preaching.** Nephi spoke much unto his brethren in the energy of his soul. They humbled themselves because of his words so that Lehi inquired of the Lord where to obtain food. (See v. 22 and 24.)

8. **Work.** Working is a great way to overcome discouragement. It not only lifts the spirit, but it can solve the problem. (See v. 19-23.)

* * *

STORY 11

NEPHI BUILDS A SHIP

Reference: 1 Nephi 17:1-55; 18:1-4

Background: *Lehi and his family journeyed in the wilderness for eight years. Though they waded through much affliction, the Lord blessed them. He gave them the Liahona (compass) to direct them. (See Story 9.) He made them strong and healthy and provided means for them to accomplish His commandments. The travelers came to a land by the seashore, which they named Bountiful because of its much fruit and honey. There they pitched their tents and rejoiced.*

Story Outline: The Lord commands Nephi to construct a ship to carry his people across the sea and shows him the manner after which it is to be built. Nephi asks the Lord where to go to find ore to molten for tools. He, then, makes a bellows, smelts the ore, and fabricates the tools.

Nephi's brothers think he is a fool to try to build a ship. They complain and mock Nephi to the point that he becomes sorrowful. They doubt that Nephi was instructed by the Lord to build a ship. They also doubt that their father, Lehi, was inspired by the Lord to lead them out of Jerusalem.

Nephi speaks to his doubting brothers. He compares their family's journey in the wilderness to the exodus of the Israelites from Egypt. He points out that the Lord did all things for the Israelites. The Lord led them by the prophet Moses, protected them, fed them, gave them water, chastened them, and healed them. Yet, the Israelites hardened their hearts. Nephi testifies that Lehi was commanded of the Lord to save his family from the destruction that is to come upon Jerusalem. He reminds his brothers that they have seen an angel and heard the voice of the Lord. He asks them why they still harden their hearts, knowing the great power of the word of God.

The brothers are angered by Nephi's words and approach him to cast him into the sea. But Nephi is so full of the Spirit and power of God that he commands them not to touch him or they will wither as a dry reed, for God will smite them. The brothers are confounded by Nephi's further admonition. He tells them to murmur no more against their father and not to withhold their labor from building the ship. For many days, they dare not lay a finger on their younger brother.

The Lord tells Nephi to stretch forth his hand to his brethren and they will not wither but will receive a shock. After being thus shaken by the Lord, the brothers confess that the Lord is with Nephi. They would worship Nephi but he forbids them and tells them to worship the Lord, which they do.

With the help of his brothers, Nephi proceeds with the ship building. He goes into the mount often to be instructed of the Lord. The ship is built not after the manner of men but after the manner shown unto Nephi by the Lord. After the ship is finished, the brothers are humbled by the exceedingly fine results.

Gospel Principles:

1. **Adversity.**
   - The Lord will support us and strengthen us in our afflictions if we keep His commandments. (See 1 Nephi 17:1-6.)

- Nephi recognized that the Lord had blessed them through their trials, but Laman and Lemuel only complained and murmured. (Compare 1 Nephi 17:1-3 with 17:20-22.)
- At times, the Lord has to use adversity to humble us and turn us to Him. (See 1 Nephi 17:41.)

2. **Attitude.**
   - Over and over again, we read of the difference in attitudes between Nephi and his brothers. Nephi was positive and full of faith. His brothers were negative and doubtful. Nephi was very willing to do as the Lord commanded. Without complaint, he set right to work making tools to build the ship. His brothers did not want to help with the work and proceeded to mock him and gripe about all their hardships in the wilderness. (Compare 1 Nephi 17:9-11 and 17:17-22.)
   - Nephi was sorrowful that his brothers were hardhearted and he sought to help them improve their attitudes. Their reaction was anger, even unto a desire to throw Nephi into the sea. (See 1 Nephi 17:47-48.)

3. **Divine guidance.**
   - If we keep His commandments, the Lord prepares the way for us to accomplish His work. (See 1 Nephi 17:3 and 5.)
   - It was the Lord who delivered Lehi and his family from the destruction of Jerusalem and guided them in the wilderness toward the promised land. (See 1 Nephi 17:12-14.) So also, it was the Lord who delivered the Israelites out of bondage in Egypt and led them through the wilderness to *their* promised land. (See 1 Nephi 17:23-32.) Do we realize how much the Lord directs our lives?

4. **Faith.**
   - Nephi displayed no doubt. His only question of the Lord was where he should go to find ore to start the work he was commanded to do. (See 1 Nephi 17:9.)

- Nephi knew that he could do all things that the Lord should command him, even unto turning water into earth. (See 1 Nephi 17:50-51.)

5. **Forgetfulness.** The brothers of Nephi were like the Israelites who were led by Moses in the wilderness. Laman and Lemuel found it easy to forget the Lord their God even after witnessing His great power. They lacked faith and hardened their hearts. (See 1 Nephi 17:30 and 45-46.)

6. **Holy Ghost.**
   - The Lord spoke to Nephi's brothers in a still small voice. But, they were past feeling; they could not feel His words. (See 1 Nephi 17:45.) Here is a key to how we should listen to the Spirit – with the feelings in our hearts. From *D&C* 8:2, "Yea, behold, I will tell you in your mind and in your heart, by the Holy Ghost, which shall come upon you and which shall dwell in your heart."
   - What a marvelous experience Nephi had in this story! He was so full of the Spirit that he was nearly consumed physically. So great was the power of the Spirit radiating from him that his brothers dared not touch him. (See 1 Nephi 17:47-48.)

7. **Obedience.** Disputation, reluctance, and hesitation were not in Nephi's character. He obeyed the Lord right away. (See 1 Nephi 17:8-9.)

8. **Power of God.** We see many examples of the power of God in this story:
   a) The marvelous works done for the Israelites in bringing them out of Egypt (see 1 Nephi 17:26-32),
   b) The creation and peopling of the earth and the ruling of nations from on high (see 1 Nephi 17:36-39),
   c) Communication to His children and control of the elements (see 1 Nephi 17:45-46),

    d) The power given to Nephi to confound his brothers and to build a ship after the manner of God (see 1 Nephi 17:48-52), and

    e) The shock or shaking given to Nephi's brothers when he stretched forth his hand as commanded by the Lord (see 1 Nephi 17:53-55).

9. **Prayer.** Nephi was called into the mountain by the voice of the Lord. There, he cried unto the Lord and was told to build a ship. Nephi returned to the mount often to pray and be instructed. (See 1 Nephi 17:7-8; 18:3.)

10. **Revelation.**
   - As did Moses, Jesus, and others, Nephi received revelation on a mountain. (See 1 Nephi 17:7-8; 18:3.)
   - Nephi listed several ways that the Lord communicates with man: by angels, by a still small voice, and by a voice of thunder and power. (See 1 Nephi 17:45-46.)
   - Man's ways and God's ways differ. (See Isaiah 55:8-9.) The ship was clearly constructed after the manner the Lord revealed to Nephi. (See 1 Nephi 18:1-2.)

11. **Reward for righteousness.** The righteous are favored of God. The land is blessed for their sakes. The Lord loves those who keep His commandments. He strengthens them so that they can do what He asks of them. Nevertheless, they will not be without trials. (See 1 Nephi 17:3, 32-38 and 40-41.)

12. **Reward for wickedness.** The Lord destroys wicked nations and curses the land against them for their sakes. (See 1 Nephi 17:32-38 and 43.)

13. **Work.** Are you like Nephi, willing to work? Or, do you prefer to complain and withhold your labor until you are compelled, like Nephi's brothers? (See 1 Nephi 17:8-11, 17-18, 48-49 and 53-54.)

14. **Worldliness.** Nephi's brothers expressed their worldly natures when they said they would rather have stayed home to enjoy their possessions. They did not believe their father was inspired nor did they understand why they had to leave Jerusalem. (See 1 Nephi 17:20-21.) To the worldly, the things of God are foolishness. (See 1 Corinthians 2:14.)

* * *

STORY 12

LEHI'S FAMILY CROSSES THE OCEAN

Reference: 1 Nephi 18:5-25

Background: *Lehi and his family were led by the Lord out of Jerusalem and through the wilderness to the seashore at Bountiful. There, the Lord commanded Nephi to build a ship. Nephi's older brothers helped him only after they were confounded by the power of God. When completed, the ship, which was built after the Lord's manner, was of fine workmanship. (See Story 11.)*

Story Outline: The Lord tells Lehi to take his family into the ship. They prepare and load their provisions, board the ship, and put forth into the sea. The wind drives them toward the promised land.

After many days at sea, Nephi's brothers and the sons of Ishmael, with their wives, take to rude merrymaking. Nephi, fearing the wrath of the Lord, attempts to call them to repentance. Laman and Lemuel become angry with him, bind him with cords, and treat him harshly.

After Nephi is bound, the compass or Liahona stops working. (See Story 9.) Consequently, the revelers do not know where to steer. A great storm arises and the ship is driven back for three days. Though they fear being drowned, the rebellious ones will not loosen Nephi's bands. The pleadings of father Lehi and Nephi's wife and children fail to soften their hearts. Lehi and his wife, Sariah, are brought down to their sickbeds by the grief and sorrow they suffer from the rudeness of their sons.

Finally, on the fourth day, after the tempest worsens and threatens their destruction, the brothers repent and loosen Nephi's bands. Though his wrists and ankles are sore and swollen, he does not murmur about his afflictions. The compass starts working again for him, and as a result of his prayers, the storm ceases.

Nephi guides the ship. After many days of sailing, the families reach the promised land. They pitch their tents and begin to cultivate and explore their new home. The land is bounteous, and they are blessed.

Gospel Principles:

1. **Attitude.** Nephi continued to praise God rather than murmur, even though he was bound until his wrists and ankles were sore. (See v. 15-16.)

2. **Forgetfulness.** Nephi's brothers forgot that it was the power of the Lord that led them. They forgot how the ship they were enjoying was built under the direction of the Lord. They turned to revelry and rudeness. (See v. 9.) It is easy to forget the Lord when things are going smoothly.

3. **Holy Ghost.** The compass acted much like the gift of the Holy Ghost does for us. If we forget God and turn to sin we lose the guidance of this divine gift. (See v. 12-13 and 21. Also see Story 9.)

4. **Honoring parents.** The behavior of Nephi's brothers brought their parents down low, nigh unto death. (See v. 17-19.) It is a natural thing for parents to grieve when their children are disobedient and contentious.

5. **Power of God.** It took the power of God, as manifest in the severe tempest, to cause the brothers to repent and free Nephi. (See v. 15 and 20.)

6. **Preparation.** Lehi's family was wise in preparing every needful thing for their journey across the sea. (See v. 6.)

7. **Repentance.** For some it takes greater stimulus to bring about repentance than for others. The brothers were so hardhearted that the pleadings of family members went unheeded. Only after the tempest worsened did Laman and Lemuel repent. (See v. 13-15 and 17-20.)

8. **Reward for wickedness.** The Lord shows forth his power against the wicked. (See v. 11-15.)

9. **Sin.** This story demonstrates how the effects of sin are spread to the sinner's family. All on the ship were in peril because of the revelry and rebellion of Nephi's brothers. Their parents and Nephi's family were particularly affected. (See v. 9-19.)

* * *

STORY 13

THE NEPHITES SEPARATE FROM THE LAMANITES

Reference: 2 Nephi 4:12-14; 5:1-28

Background: *After crossing the sea, Lehi and his family settled in the promised land. (See Story 12.) Lehi, waxing old, gave counsel and blessings to all of his household. (See 2 Nephi 1 through 3.)*

Story Outline: Father Lehi dies and is buried. Laman, Lemuel, and the sons of Ishmael become angry at Nephi because he admonishes them to follow the Lord. They refuse to allow their younger brother to rule over them. Their anger increases to the point that they seek to take away Nephi's life.

The Lord warns Nephi to take those who will go with him and flee into the wilderness. Calling themselves the people of Nephi, all those who believe in the revelations of God depart with Nephi. Included are his sisters, some of his brothers (Sam, Jacob, and Joseph), and Zoram (see Story 4) with all of their families. The people of Nephi separate themselves by a journey of many days into the wilderness. They pitch their tents and settle in a place, which they call Nephi.

The people of Nephi keep the commandments of God and are prospered by the Lord. They grow crops, raise herds, and multiply in the land. Nephi, their leader, teaches them to make swords, build buildings, and work with wood and metals. A temple is built. Nephi's younger brothers, Jacob and Joseph, are consecrated by Nephi to be priests and teachers. The Nephites become an industrious and happy people.

Meanwhile, those who stayed with Laman and Lemuel harden their hearts against God, are cursed, and receive a skin of blackness. Because of their cursing, they become an idle people, full of mischief and subtlety, hunting beasts of prey for their living. The Lord tells Nephi that these, his brethren, now called Lamanites (see 2 Nephi 5:14), will be used as a scourge (see 2 Nephi 5:25) to stir up his people, the Nephites (see 2 Nephi 29:12; Jacob 1:13-14), in remembrance of the Lord.

Gospel Principles:

1. **Choosing the right.** Much like the spirits in the premortal war in heaven, Lehi's posterity had to choose whom they would follow. (Compare 2 Nephi 5:6 with 2 Nephi 5:20.) Each day we make choices as to which voices we will heed.

2. **Happiness.** The people of Nephi lived in happiness because their lives were in harmony with the commandments of the Lord. They organized the Church, built a temple, increased their education, and were industrious. (See 2 Nephi 5:10-17 and 26-27.)

3. **Industry.** The people of Nephi were actively engaged in good works: raising crops and animals, building buildings, and working with wood and metals. Their life style was after the manner of happiness. (See 2 Nephi 5:10-17 and 27.) Contrast their industry with the idleness of the Lamanites who cut themselves off from the Lord. (See 2 Nephi 5:20-24.)

4. **Jealousy.** Nephi's elder brethren refused to humble themselves and submit to the rule of their younger brother in the Lord. Their

jealousy and anger increased and led them to murderous desires. (See 2 Nephi 5:2-3.)

5. **Leadership.** Nephi's attitude about leadership is apparent. His effort was not for his own sake and glory, but for the good of his people to protect them and make them happy. He did not desire to be their king, but he did for them that which was in his power, teaching and leading them. (See 2 Nephi 5:15-19; Jacob 1:10.)

6. **Opposition.** The principle of opposition in all things, as taught by Lehi to Jacob (see 2 Nephi 2:11-18), is demonstrated by the polarization of these two nations out of the same family.

7. **Preparation.** Nephi had the insight to prepare his people to defend themselves. He taught them to perform productive labor. (See 2 Nephi 5:14-15.)

8. **Records.** It is significant that the people of Nephi brought with them the records engraved upon the plates of brass. By so doing, they were able to know, remember, and keep the commandments of the Lord. (See 2 Nephi 5:10 and 12.)

9. **Remembrance.** The Lord said He would use the Lamanites as a scourge to help the Nephites remember Him. (See 2 Nephi 5:25.)

10. **Revelation.** The Lord warned Nephi to depart from his murderous brethren. (See 2 Nephi 5:5-6.) Are we, like Nephi, receptive and responsive to the warnings that the Lord gives us?

11. **Slothfulness.** The Lamanites hardened their hearts against God and became an idle people. Not being engaged in industry like the Nephites, they had time to be full of mischief and subtlety. (See 2 Nephi 5:24.)

* * *

SHEREM DENIES CHRIST

Reference: Jacob 7:1-23

Background: *Nephi and all those who believed in the revelations of God separated themselves from Laman and Lemuel, who refused to be ruled by their younger brother and sought to take away his life. The people of Nephi settled in the land of Nephi. Jacob and Joseph, Nephi's younger brothers, were consecrated to be priests and teachers. (See Story 13.) Before his death, Nephi charged Jacob to write that which was sacred on the small plates. (See Jacob 1:1-4, 12 and 18. Also see Story 8.)*

Story Outline: Sherem comes amongst the people of Nephi preaching that there shall be no Christ. He is learned and skilled in language. Using flattery and powerful speech, Sherem leads many away from Christ.

Sherem seeks out Jacob with the intent to destroy his faith. He accuses Jacob of preaching false doctrine concerning the coming of Christ. By the Spirit, Jacob confounds Sherem, pointing out that the scriptures testify of Christ and bearing personal witness of the need for the atonement.

Sherem asks for a sign of the power of the Holy Ghost. Jacob replies that if the Lord wills to give him a sign he will be smitten. At those words, Sherem collapses.

After several days of being nourished, Sherem requests an audience with the people before he dies. He addresses the multitude and denies the things he taught them. He confesses the reality of Christ and admits that he was deceived by the power of the Devil. Then, Sherem dies.

In answer to Jacob's prayers, the multitude is overcome by the power of God after witnessing Sherem's confession. Peace and the love of God are restored amongst the people.

Gospel Principles:

1. **Deception.**
   • Because of Sherem's knowledge of the language, his powerful speech, and use of flattery, he was able to lead many away. (See v. 2 and 4.) Even today, seemingly learned people try to deceive us.
   • Before his death, Sherem admitted that he had been deceived by the Devil. (See v. 18-19.)

2. **Holy Ghost.**
   • It was by the power of the Holy Ghost that Jacob was able to confound Sherem. By the same power, Jacob had obtained his testimony of Christ and the atonement. (See v. 8 and 12-13.)
   • In the end, Sherem confessed the power of the Holy Ghost. (See v. 17.)

3. **Opposition.**
   • Sherem was anxious to shake Jacob's faith. (See v. 3.) If you have a testimony and are trying to live the gospel, you can expect to meet opposition that will try to drag you down.
   • Sherem's confession points out the conflict between the two great opposing powers of Christ and Satan. (Contrast v. 17 with v. 18.)

4. **Power of God.** Sherem confessed the power of God only after being struck down. He should not have tempted God. (See v. 14-17.)

5. **Prophets.** All of the prophets have spoken concerning Christ. (See v. 11.)

6. **Reward for wickedness.** Sherem had cause to fear greatly because he had lied to God and deceived many. (See v. 18-19.)

7. **Satan.** The Devil has power to deceive. He uses that power of deception to draw people away from Christ. (See v. 4 and 18.)

8. **Scriptures.** The scriptures testify of Jesus Christ. Studying the scriptures will help us keep from being led astray. (See v. 10-11 and 23.)

9. **Steadfastness.** Jacob stood firm in his faith. By the power of the Holy Ghost he withstood Sherem's attempt to shake him. (See v. 5, 8 and 12.)

10. **Testimony.** Jacob's testimony was strong. Because of the many revelations and manifestations he had received, he could not be shaken. (See v. 3, 5 and 12.)

11. **Vanity.** Sherem played on the people's vanity by using flattery. (See v. 2 and 4.)

* * *

STORY 15

ENOS PRAYS ALL DAY

Reference: Enos 1:1-19

Background: *Enos was the son of Jacob who was Nephi's younger brother. Jacob passed the plates to Enos. (See Jacob 7:27.)*

Story Outline: Enos goes hunting in the forest and ponders the eternal things his father has taught him. He kneels and prays mightily all day and into the night. Enos hears a voice, and his sins are forgiven. He then prays for the welfare of his brethren, the Nephites. After receiving an answer, Enos has faith to pray for his enemies, the Lamanites. He receives the promise that a record will be preserved to bring the Lamanites unto salvation in the Lord's own due time. After this experience, Enos goes amongst the people of Nephi prophesying and testifying.

Gospel Principles:

1. **Faith.**
   - Enos was forgiven because of his faith in Christ whom he had never heard nor seen. (See v. 8.) We need the same kind of faith today.
   - Enos' faith grew in strength as he prevailed with the Lord. First he prayed for himself, then for the Nephites, then for the Lamanites. He asked in faith, in the name of Christ, believing

that he would receive. Then Enos' soul could rest because he knew the Lord would keep His promise to preserve the records for the Lamanites. (See v. 6, 11 and 15-18.)

2. **Forgiveness.** Enos' repentance was complete and his guilt was swept away. (See v. 5-6.) Sometimes we fail to forgive ourselves after the Lord has forgiven us.

3. **Journals.** Enos, as well as his fathers, desired and were granted that the records would be preserved for future generations. (See v. 13 and 18.) The records we keep can benefit our descendants.

4. **Love.** Enos showed his love for his fellow men by earnestly praying for them, first for his brethren, the Nephites, and then for his enemies, the Lamanites.

5. **Mercy.**
   • The Lord gave Lehi's descendants this holy land for an inheritance. (See v. 10.)
   • The promise to preserve the records for the salvation of future generations shows the love and mercy that God has for His children. (See v. 16.)

6. **Parenthood.** Enos' father spoke to him often about eternal things. The teachings of his father prompted Enos to pray in the forest. (See v. 1 and 3.)

7. **Pondering.** The words of eternal life sunk deep into the heart of Enos. This pondering filled him with desire to seek the Lord. (See v. 3-4.)

8. **Prayer.** Have you ever been earnest enough in your prayers to continue for a whole day and on into the night? (See v. 4.)

9. **Records.** Enos understood the importance of the records, that they could be a means of bringing salvation to future generations. (See v. 13-14.)

10. **Repentance.**
    - Enos described his repentance as a wrestle before God. (See v. 2 and 4).
    - After earnest prayer, as part of his repentance, Enos felt the acceptance that comes from being forgiven of the Lord. (See v. 5-6.)

11. **Reward for wickedness.** Iniquity will bring a curse upon this land. (See v. 10.)

12. **Spirituality.** Enos hungered for spiritual food more than for the fruits of hunting beasts. (See v. 4.)

13. **Testimony.** Enos knew that his father had a knowledge of the gospel, but he strove to gain his own personal testimony through prayer and faith.

14. **Warning.** At the time of Enos, the people were so stiffnecked that the prophets had to threaten and warn to keep them off the path of destruction. (See v. 22-23.)

* * *

STORY 16

MOSIAH DISCOVERS ZARAHEMLA AND THE MULEKITES

Reference: Omni 1:12-19

Background: *The records (plates), kept and added to significantly by Nephi and Jacob, were passed on to Enos to Jarom to Omni to Amaron to Chemish to Abinadom and to Amaleki. Each man added a few words about the life in the land of Nephi in his days. There were seasons of war, seasons of peace, wicked men, righteous men, contentions, judgments, and destructions. Amaleki was born in the days of Mosiah who became king over the land of Zarahemla.*

Story Outline: Mosiah, warned of the Lord to leave the land of Nephi, takes with him into the wilderness those who will hearken unto the Lord. They are led by preaching and prophesying until they discover the land of Zarahemla. The people of Zarahemla are the Mulekites, who came out of Jerusalem at the time King Zedekiah was carried away captive into Babylon.

Because the people of Zarahemla brought no records with them, their language is corrupted, and they deny the existence of their Creator. Mosiah has them taught in his language so that they can communicate together. Zarahemla then tells his genealogy from memory, and it is written in the records.

The two peoples unite and appoint Mosiah to be their king.

Gospel Principles:

1. **Communication.** Until the two peoples could speak the same language they could not become united.

2. **Genealogy.** After Zarahemla was taught in the language of Mosiah he could give his genealogy and have it written down. (See v. 18.) Has someone recorded your genealogy?

3. **Obedience.** Those who would hearken to the Lord were obedient and left the land of Nephi. They heeded the warning that Mosiah had received. (See v. 12-13.)

4. **Records.** Without the anchor of written records, the language and faith of the Mulekites drifted away from the standard. (See v. 17.) In our public schools we learn our language. But, many people are adrift in their belief in God because they do not read and study the Standard Works.

5. **Unity.**
   - Since only those who would hearken to the Lord went with Mosiah, they were united in purpose and were led by the Lord. (See v. 13.)
   - Zarahemla rejoiced that the Lord sent Mosiah and his people with the plates. After the people of Zarahemla were taught his language, they gladly united under Mosiah's leadership. (See v. 14 and 19.)

* * *

STORY 17

KING BENJAMIN REIGNS IN RIGHTEOUSNESS

Reference: Words of Mormon 1:12-18

Background: *Amaleki, keeper of the records, saw the death of Mosiah, king over the people of Zarahemla. (See Story 16.) He also saw the subsequent reign of Mosiah's son, Benjamin. Amaleki delivered the small plates to King Benjamin who put them with the other records. (See Omni 1:23-25.)*

Many years later, Mormon attached the small plates to his abridgement of the large plates for a special purpose known to God. (See Story 8 and Words of Mormon 1:9-11.) Both sets of Nephi's plates, small and large, cover the period up to the reign of King Benjamin. (See Words of Mormon 1:3.)

Story Outline: In the days of King Benjamin there are external and internal contentions and conflicts. The armies of the Lamanites come out of the land of Nephi against his people in Zarahemla. By exercising the strength of himself, his people, and the Lord, Benjamin drives the Lamanites out of their land.

False Christs, false prophets, and false preachers and teachers arise and are punished according to their crimes. King Benjamin, a holy man, reigns in righteousness. He enlists the help of the holy prophets in the land, labors with all his might, and establishes peace in Zarahemla.

Gospel Principles:

1. **Attitude.** We do not read of Benjamin becoming discouraged by his many problems, only of him working to overcome them.

2. **Diligence.** King Benjamin persisted until all obstacles were removed and peace was established. (See v. 18.)

3. **Example.** Benjamin fought with his own arm. He was a holy man, an example to his people. (See v. 13 and 17.)

4. **Leadership.** The King was able to rally his armies against the enemies without and enlist the assistance of prophets to correct the strife within. In righteousness, he led his people in the strength of the Lord. (See v. 14.)

* * *

STORY 18

KING BENJAMIN TEACHES HIS SONS

Reference: Mosiah 1:1-8

Background: *King Benjamin, with the help of his people in Zarahemla, overcame external attacks by the Lamanites and internal contentions from false prophets. (See Story 17.) His reign was concluded in continual peace.*

Story Outline: Benjamin causes his three sons, Mosiah, Helorum, and Helaman, to be taught in the language of his fathers. He teaches them to be men of understanding, to know of the prophecies and the records on the plates of brass. (See Story 4.) Without the records, their people would have dwindled in unbelief and ignorance. Benjamin enjoins his sons to search the plates and keep the commandments that they may prosper in the land.

Gospel Principles:

1. **Family home evening.** The record does not state, but we wonder what the setting was for the King to teach his sons. Was it some form of a family home evening? Certainly, that is a forum we have been advised to use in this day to teach our children.

2. **Parenthood.**
   - King Benjamin recognized the importance of teaching his sons many things that they might become men of understanding. Particularly, he realized the importance of teaching them the prophecies and commandments of God.
   - Lehi and Benjamin carried on a tradition of parents teaching their children from generation to generation. (See v. 4.)

3. **Records.** The written records were essential in teaching the posterity of Lehi. Without the records much would have been forgotten. (See v. 4.)

4. **Reward for righteousness.** We profit from searching the scriptures. Those who keep the commandments will prosper in the land. (See v. 7.)

5. **Scriptures.** Benjamin realized that without the scriptures people dwindle in unbelief. We have the scriptures, but if we do not search them, we are no better off than those who do not have them. (See v. 3-5 and 7.)

6. **Teaching.** The wise king taught his sons many things. Of utmost importance were the things he taught them from the scriptures. (See v. 4 and 8.)

* * *

STORY 19

KING BENJAMIN
ADDRESSES HIS PEOPLE

Reference: Mosiah 1:9-18; 2:1-8; 4:1-4; 5:1-8; 6:1-3

Background: *Benjamin, righteous king of the people in Zarahemla, taught his three sons to be men of understanding. (See Story 18.)*

Story Outline: Realizing that he has become old, King Benjamin tells his son, Mosiah, to call the people together with a proclamation that Benjamin might address them. He gives Mosiah charge of the affairs of the kingdom and of the records.

The people of Zarahemla gather to hear the words of their king. They bring sacrifices to be offered to the Lord in thanksgiving for their good leaders who have brought them peace. Great in number, the people pitch their tents by families around the temple.

Benjamin has a tower built so that he can address such a great multitude. He causes his words to be written and passed amongst those who cannot hear his voice. His counsel covers many topics:

a) King Benjamin's purpose is to unfold the mysteries of God, not to boast nor exalt himself. He has brought civil order and has labored with his own hands to serve rather than burden his people. Benjamin wants to clear his conscience of his responsibility to teach his people and to declare his son, Mosiah, to be their king. (See Mosiah 2:9-15 and 26-31.)

b) Service to others is service to God. (See Mosiah 2:16-19.)

c) The Lord blesses us more than we can ever repay through all our service. Even if we serve God continually, we will still be in His debt because He blesses us so much for our service. (See Mosiah 2:20-25.)

d) Beware of contentions that come from listening to and obeying the Evil One. (See Mosiah 2:32-33.)

e) Those who knowingly transgress the laws of God withdraw themselves from the Spirit of the Lord. If they do not repent, they must suffer a never-ending torment. (See Mosiah 2:34-40; 3:23-27.)

f) Those who keep God's commandments and endure to the end will dwell with God in never-ending happiness. (See Mosiah 2:41.)

g) Benjamin prophesies of the Savior's ministry, suffering, and atonement. (See Mosiah 3:1-11.)

h) Repentance and forgiveness are possible only through Christ. The law of Moses, the many signs, and the holy prophets are meaningless without the atonement of Christ's blood. (See Mosiah 3:12-22.)

i) The natural man is an enemy to God. (See Mosiah 3:19.)

King Benjamin finishes speaking and observes that his people have fallen to the earth in fear of the Lord. They cry for mercy and forgiveness through the atoning blood of Christ. The Spirit of the Lord comes upon them and fills them with joy. Benjamin speaks to them again:

j) Always remember the greatness of God and your own nothingness. (See Mosiah 4:5-11.)

k) Be humble, pray daily, remain faithful, and you will rejoice and retain a remission of your sins. You will be filled with love, live in peace, teach your children to love, serve and live in truth, succor the needy, and impart of your substance to others. (See Mosiah 4:11-30.)

King Benjamin sends amongst his people to know if they believe his words. Their reply is that they believe, even to the extent that their hearts are changed. They desire no more to do evil, only good continually. They are willing to enter into a covenant to obey God's commandments for the rest of their lives. Benjamin commends them for their righteous covenant by which they become spiritually begotten children of Christ. He continues teaching them:

1) Take upon yourselves the name of Christ. Salvation and freedom come only through His name. (See Mosiah 5:7-15.)

After King Benjamin finishes speaking to the people, he takes the names of those who enter into the covenant with God to keep His commandments. With only the exception of the little children, all enter.

Benjamin consecrates Mosiah to be king and appoints priests to teach the people. The multitude is dismissed, and they return to their homes.

Gospel Principles:

1. **Commitment.**
   - The multitude was willing to make a covenant to keep God's commandments. Benjamin recorded their names to confirm their commitment. (See Mosiah 5:2 and 5; 6:1-3.)
   - The test is in carrying out the covenants we make. Have you ever been filled with the Spirit at a meeting, enthused and willing to do nothing but good continually, only to find yourself back to your old bad habits the next day? It takes real

commitment to make the mighty change in your heart be a permanent improvement of your life.

2. **Communication.** King Benjamin was a good communicator. He went the extra mile to make sure his message got through by erecting a tower so that more people could hear and by sending written word amongst those who could not hear his voice. He followed up by sending amongst the people to see if the message was received. He spoke by the Spirit, and, to his joy, the word was received by the Spirit. (See Mosiah 2:7-9; 5:1-2 and 6.)

3. **Covenants.** After hearing King Benjamin's address and experiencing a change of heart, the people were willing to enter into a covenant with God to keep His commandments for the rest of their lives. (See Mosiah 5:4-8.)

4. **Faith.** The people had faith on Benjamin's words. They believed in Jesus Christ, that through His atoning blood their sins could be forgiven. Through their faith, King Benjamin's people received peace of conscience and great joy. Their hearts were changed and they entered into a covenant with God. (See Mosiah 4:2-3; 5:1-4.)

5. **Forgiveness.** Through their faith, the people received a remission of their sins and peace of mind. Their hearts were changed and they were spiritually begotten of Christ through whom they were made free. How sweet is the blessing of forgiveness! (See Mosiah 4:3; 5:7-8.)

6. **Holy Ghost.** The major roles of the Holy Ghost are demonstrated in this story: to comfort, to confirm the truth, and to reveal knowledge. After the people had repented, the Spirit of the Lord filled them with joy, giving them peace of conscience through remission of sins. By the Spirit they knew that Benjamin's words were true, their hearts were changed, and they were given views of the future. (See Mosiah 4:3; 5:2-3.)

7. **Joy.** The people were filled with joy because of their faith, the forgiveness of their sins, and the peace and knowledge given them by the Holy Ghost. (See Mosiah 4:3; 5:4.)

8. **Leadership.** The people were thankful to have a just man to be their king. Benjamin established peace in the land and taught them to keep the commandments. (See Mosiah 2:4.)

9. **Peace.** Peace of conscience was the fruit of their faith and forgiveness. True peace comes through the Holy Ghost from living our lives in harmony with God's commandments. (See Mosiah 4:3.)

10. **Preaching.**
    • The preaching of King Benjamin brought about a great change in his people. They committed themselves to do good continually and keep all of God's commandments. (See Mosiah 5:2 and 5.)
    • This wise king realized that the people would need reminding of their covenant so he appointed priests to teach them. (See Mosiah 6:3.)

11. **Prophecy.** The people of King Benjamin were so full of the Spirit that they could see into the future and could prophesy if it was expedient. (See Mosiah 5:3.) In a related *Old Testament* story, Moses wished that all men were prophets. (See Numbers 11:27-29.)

12. **Repentance.** This story demonstrates the steps to repentance. Benjamin's speech made the multitude recognize their sins and feel remorse, even fear. By exercising faith in the Savior, they were forgiven and obtained peace of conscience. Their hearts were truly changed; by the Spirit they were born again and lost their desire to do evil. They committed themselves with a covenant to keep all of the commandments from that time forth. (See Mosiah 4:1-3; 5:2, 5 and 7.)

13. **Service.** King Benjamin labored with his own hands so that he would not be a burden on his people. He taught them by word and exemplary deed that service to fellow man is service to God. (See Mosiah 2:16-19.)

* * *

STORY 20

AMMON RETURNS TO
THE LAND OF NEPHI

Reference: Mosiah 7:1-33; 8:1-5; 21:18-19 and 22-24

Background: *King Benjamin lived for three more years after addressing the people of Zarahemla and conferring the kingdom upon his son, Mosiah. (See Story 19.) For the first three years of righteous King Mosiah's reign, there was continual peace amongst all the people. (See Mosiah 6:4-7.)*

Amaleki (see Story 16) had spoken of some people who had tried to return to the land of Nephi to possess the lands of their inheritance. Their strong leader caused a contention, and all but fifty of their party were slain in the wilderness. The fifty survivors returned to Zarahemla. Zeniff gathered others and took them into the wilderness. (See Story 21.) Amaleki heard nothing concerning them after that. (See Omni 1:27-30.)

Story Outline: Mosiah and his people in Zarahemla desire to know what has become of Zeniff and his people who returned to the land of Nephi (also known as the land of Lehi-Nephi). A party of sixteen, strong men, under Ammon's leadership, is sent out to find their departed brethren. The party wanders for forty days in the wilderness looking for the land of Nephi.

Ammon and three of his brethren leave the main camp and go into the land of Nephi. Near the walls of the city Lehi-Nephi, they are captured by the local king's guards who are outside the city with the King.

After two days of imprisonment, Ammon is brought before the King who introduces himself as Limhi, son of Noah, who was the son of Zeniff who came out of Zarahemla. Ammon explains who he is and why he came. King Limhi rejoices to hear that his brethren in Zarahemla are alive. He looks to them to free his people from the bondage and grievous taxation enforced by the Lamanites. For fear of the Lamanites, King Limhi does not even dare to go outside of the city without having his guards with him.

Limhi gathers his people together the next day and addresses them. He admonishes them to trust in the Lord for deliverance, reminding them that their bondage is a result of their iniquity.

After the King finishes speaking, he has Ammon tell the multitude all about what has happened in Zarahemla since Zeniff left there. Ammon also expounds upon King Benjamin's last address.

The plates containing the history of the people in the land of Nephi since they left Zarahemla are brought to Ammon to read. (Stories 21 through 27 cover that history.)

Gospel Principles:

1. **Bondage.** Zeniff was over-zealous to inherit the land of his fathers, so he entered into a treaty with the Lamanite King Laman, which led him and his people into bondage. (See Mosiah 7:21-22.) Similarly, our zeal to obtain a certain end may lead us to embrace some seemingly harmless practice that eventually binds us deeply in sin.

2. **Brotherhood.** There was a strong bond and feeling of brotherhood between the two groups of Nephites who had been long separated

from each other. Limhi's joy was great when he discovered that the people of Zarahemla were alive and had sent representatives to him and his people. (See Mosiah 7:14.)

3. **Humility.** Much like the Prodigal Son who returned to his father, Limhi was willing to submit to slavery at the hands of the Nephites in Zarahemla to escape the Lamanite captivity. (See Mosiah 7:15.)

4. **Lost sheep.** It was the desire to know of their brethren that drove Mosiah to send the expedition to the land of Nephi. Limhi and his people were full of joy to be found and given hope of deliverance. (See Mosiah 7:1-2 and 13-15.)

5. **Records.** Records were kept by the people who left Zarahemla. Thus, Ammon could read of their history, and so can we. (See Mosiah 8:5.)

6. **Reward for righteousness.** Limhi's advice to his people to turn to the Lord for deliverance can apply to us today. It is only through trusting and serving the Lord that we can escape the bondage of sin. (See Mosiah 7:33.)

7. **Reward for wickedness.** Limhi pointed out that the transgressions of his people had brought them into their grievous bondage. (See Mosiah 7:20-32.)

8. **Trust in God.** Limhi's counsel to his people was to trust in God who brought Israel out of Egypt and led Lehi out of Jerusalem. He told them to turn to the Lord with full purpose of heart. (See Mosiah 7:19-20 and 33.)

9. **Welfare.** King Limhi was concerned for the welfare of the men left outside the city walls who had journeyed with Ammon. The King brought them into the city and gave them food, drink, and rest. (See Mosiah 7:16.)

* * *

STORY 21

ZENIFF GOES UP TO POSSESS
THE LAND OF NEPHI

Reference: Mosiah 9:1-19; 10:1-22; 7:21-22

Background: *Amaleki (see Story 16) had written about the people who left Zarahemla to possess the land of their inheritance, the land of Nephi. (See Omni 1:27-30.) Years later, Ammon went from Zarahemla to search for these people. He discovered King Limhi and his people in captivity. (See Story 20.) Ammon read the plates that gave an account of King Limhi's people from the time they left Zarahemla with Zeniff and settled in the land of Nephi. This story begins the history taken from those plates.*

Story Outline: Zeniff goes with the Nephite army that leaves Zarahemla to possess the land of Nephi. He is sent as a spy amongst the Lamanites. Because of the good that he sees, Zeniff argues with his brethren not to destroy the Lamanites. The contention turns into a civil battle with much bloodshed. The fifty survivors return to Zarahemla.

Zeniff's zeal to inherit the land of his fathers compels him to collect those who will follow him and try another journey into the wilderness. After wandering and suffering afflictions, the party camps outside the city occupied by the Lamanites. Zeniff and four men enter the city and talk to the Lamanite King Laman. The King allows Zeniff to possess the lands of Lehi-Nephi and Shilom. However, Laman's crafty intent is to bring Zeniff's people into bondage.

The Nephites rebuild the cities, raise crops, multiply, and prosper in the land of Nephi. After twelve years, King Laman grows uneasy and stirs the Lamanites up against the Nephites.

The Nephites retaliate in battle. Because they rely upon the Lord they succeed in defeating and driving out the Lamanites. Zeniff causes his people to be industrious, to raise crops, make clothes, and prepare weapons for defense. The people of Zeniff live in peace for 22 years.

Laman, the King of the Lamanites, dies. The successor to the throne, his son, prepares the Lamanites to battle against the Nephites. Through the use of spies, Zeniff is able to prepare his people to meet their ferocious attackers. In the strength of the Lord the Nephites once again drive their enemies out of the land. Zeniff realizes that King Laman deceived him with fair promises that the Lamanites might bring the Nephites into bondage and take from them their increase. When Zeniff is old, he confers the kingdom upon his son, Noah.

Gospel Principles:

1. **Bondage.** It was the deceit used by the King of the Lamanites that brought the Nephites into bondage. (See Mosiah 7:21-22; 9:10-13.) People do not willingly give up their freedom. Today's temptations and addictions would bring us into bondage also by deceit.

2. **Deception.** Zeniff allowed himself to be deceived. His zeal to possess the land, in a sense, blinded him. (See Mosiah 7:21-22; 9:1; 10:18.) It is possible to want something so badly that one cannot clearly see the consequences.

3. **Hardheartedness.** As Zeniff explained, the Lamanites did not understand the dealings of the Lord. They knew only the arm of flesh. In their minds, Nephi and his descendants had continually wronged them. Thus, the Lamanites had built up an "eternal hatred" toward the people of the Lord. (See Mosiah 10:11-18.) Many inactive church members today hold grudges and hatred for wrongs they perceive have been done to them.

4. **Industry.** The industrious labor of Zeniff's people brought them prosperity. (See Mosiah 9:8-9; 10:4-5.)

5. **Leadership.** The severe discipline exercised by the leader of the first group of explorers was the cause of bloodshed and failure. Here is an example of poor leadership. (See Mosiah 9:2; Omni 1:28.)

6. **Maturity.** In this story we see the development of Zeniff's character and wisdom. He began as a zealous youth, overly anxious to possess the land of Nephi, unwise to the snare that the Lamanite king set for him. With time, he increased in wisdom as a righteous leader, preparing for the defense of his people, encouraging them to be industrious, and stimulating them to trust in the Lord in battle. (See Mosiah 9:3; 10:1-2, 4-5, 7 and 18-19.)

7. **Preparation.** Zeniff was wise to prepare his people against attack from the Lamanites with weapons, guards, and spies. (See Mosiah 10:1-2 and 7.)

8. **Reward for wickedness.** Zeniff realized that his afflictions in the wilderness resulted from being slow to remember God. (See Mosiah 9:3.)

9. **Sin.** A parallel can be drawn between the Lamanites and sin. At first the ways of the Lamanites looked attractive to Zeniff; he did not perceive them as enemies. King Laman deceived Zeniff by making concessions to the Nephites so that he could

take advantage of them later. (See Mosiah 7:21-22; 9:1 and 10-12; 10:18.) Even so, Satan will lie and deceive. He will make sin look exciting and attractive, will even compromise to attain his end of bringing man into bondage. Satan seeks to make all men "miserable like unto himself" (2 Nephi 2:27).

10. **Slothfulness.** The Lamanites wanted something for nothing. They wanted to glut themselves on the fruit of the labors of the captive Nephites. (See Mosiah 9:12.)

11. **Trust in God.** The people of Zeniff exercised their faith and placed their trust in God to deliver them out of the hands of their enemies. The strength of the Lord was with them and they were able to defeat the Lamanites who relied only upon their own strength. (See Mosiah 9:17-18; 10:10-11 and 19-20.)

* * *

STORY 22

KING NOAH TURNS HIS KINGDOM TO WICKEDNESS

Reference: Mosiah 11:1-29

Background: *Zeniff left Zarahemla and settled with his followers in the land of Nephi. As their king, he caused them to be industrious and prepared them to defend themselves against the Lamanites whom they defeated in the strength of the Lord. Zeniff conferred the kingdom upon his son, Noah. (See Story 21.)*

Story Outline: Noah does not follow the ways of his father. He leads an indulgent life, pursuing his own desires, not keeping the commandments of God. He also causes his people to commit sin. The flattering words of the King and his wicked priests turn the people to idolatry. They also become wine-bibbers.

The people are taxed to provide support for King Noah and his priests with all their wives and concubines. The taxes are used to construct elegant and spacious buildings, including a palace and high towers. Thus, the King and his priests sustain their pride, laziness, idolatry, whoredoms, and riotous living with the labors of the people.

The Lamanites begin raiding Noah's people, killing small groups of them and stealing their flocks. The King sends his armies out and drives back the Lamanites. The Nephites become lifted up in pride at their victory, boasting in their own strength, delighting in the shedding of blood.

The Lord sends Abinadi amongst the Nephites to call them to repentance lest they should be brought into bondage. The people are angered by Abinadi's words and seek to take his life. But, the Lord delivers him out of their hands. (See Story 23.)

Gospel Principles:

1. **Leadership.** King Noah is an example of wicked leadership. Unlike King Benjamin, who labored with his own hands for his support (see Story 19), Noah taxed his people so he could live extravagantly. By appointing proud, wicked priests, he led his people deep into sin. His focus was upon riches, buildings, status, and riotous living, not upon the people he led. (See v. 2-15.)

2. **Pride.**
   - Pride seeks its own. Noah appointed priests who shared his pride and his taste for wickedness. (See v. 5 and 8-14.)
   - Because of their victory over the Lamanites, Noah's people became lifted up in the pride of their own strength. They boasted of themselves, giving no credit to the Lord. (See v. 18-19.) What a difference from the trust in God this same people showed under Zeniff's leadership. (See Story 21.)
   - The King was so lifted up in pride that he asked, "Who is the Lord, that shall bring upon my people such great affliction?" (See v. 27.)

3. **Prophets.** Such was the state of the people's wickedness, that the Lord sent Abinadi to warn them of the consequences of continued sinning, to call them to repentance. (See v. 20-26.)

4. **Repentance.** The people were commanded to repent or the Lord would visit them in His anger. (See v. 20-25.)

5. **Selfishness.** The lives of King Noah and his wicked priests were centered upon selfish indulgence at the expense of their subjects. (See v. 3-4 and 14.)

6. **Sin.** Sin grew like a cancer in King Noah's society. The list of sins includes: selfishness, laziness, worldliness, pride, lying, flattery, whoredoms, idolatry, wine bibbing, boasting, delighting in the shedding of blood, anger, and attempted murder of a prophet. (See v. 1-15, 19 and 26-28.)

7. **Slothfulness.** Noah and his priests in their laziness supported themselves through taxation of the people. (See v. 3-4 and 6.)

8. **Worldliness.** The leaders of the Nephites did not follow the commandments of God but pursued their own desires: riches, possessions, status, and riotous living. (See v. 2, 9, 11 and 14.)

* * *

STORY 23

ABINADI TESTIFIES
BEFORE KING NOAH

Reference: Mosiah 11:20-29; 12:1-37; 13:1-35; 17:1-20

Background: *Noah, son of Zeniff, was a wicked king over the Nephites in the land of Nephi. He, with his evil priests, caused his people to support and commit all manner of sins. (See Story 22.)*

Story Outline: Abinadi is commanded by the Lord to go amongst the people of Noah to tell them that unless they repent of their wickedness they will be brought into bondage by their enemies. His prophesying falls on deafened ears and hardened hearts. Unrepentant, King Noah and his people are angry with Abinadi and seek to take his life. But, the Lord delivers him out of their hands.

After two years, Abinadi returns to prophesy to them again. He tells them that because they have not repented, the Lord will visit them in His anger with bondage, famine, pestilence, and other afflictions. Abinadi prophesies that King Noah's life will be as a garment in a hot furnace.

Angered by Abinadi's words, the people bind the prophet and bring him before the King. They claim that he has wrongly prophesied evil against them, since they believe themselves and Noah to be guiltless.

Abinadi is cast into prison and then brought before the King and his priests for questioning. Abinadi answers boldly and confounds his interrogators in their words.

King Noah commands that Abinadi be slain. The priests try to lay their hands on him, but he withstands them by the power of God, commanding them not to touch him until he finishes delivering his divine message. The Spirit of the Lord is so strong on Abinadi that his face shines, and Noah's people dare not touch him. Abinadi prophesies that what they do to him will be a type of things to come. Then he preaches to them about the Ten Commandments and the Law of Moses. Abinadi explains that without the atonement by the Messiah all will perish. He tells of the resurrection and redemption of mankind through Christ and again calls on all to repent.

When Abinadi is finished speaking, King Noah commands his priests to put him to death. Alma, one of the priests, realizes the truth of the prophet's words and pleads for him to be spared. But, the king's anger increases. He casts Alma out and sends men to slay him. Alma flees and hides.

Abinadi is cast back into prison. After three days, he is again brought before King Noah where he is sentenced to death by fire. Abinadi testifies that his words are true and that his blood will stand as a testimony against the King. Noah almost releases him for the fear of God's judgement, but his priests appeal to his vanity.

Abinadi suffers death by fire. While dying, he prophesies that the seed of his executioners will destroy other believers in God, and that his executioners will be scattered, afflicted with disease, hunted, and finally, also put to death by fire.

Gospel Principles:

1. **Atonement.** Abinadi taught Noah and his people the relationship between the Law of Moses and the atonement. He understood

well the eternal plan and mission of the Messiah many years before Christ came to the earth to live. (See Mosiah 13:27-35. Also see Mosiah 14-16.)

2. **Blindness, Spiritual.**
   - The people of Noah were so steeped in sin that they refused to see what the Lord was telling them through Abinadi. (See Story 22.) They even imagined themselves to be guiltless. Noah accused Abinadi of being mad. The wicked people just could not see their own state. (See Mosiah 11:26-29; 12:13-15; 13:1.)
   - Abinadi pointed out that the children of Israel were blind to the prophecies of Moses concerning the coming of the Messiah. (See Mosiah 13:32-35.)

3. **Courage.** Abinadi had the courage to carry out the Lord's errand even though it meant his death. He knew that the people wanted to kill him before he returned to the land of Nephi, yet he allowed them to take him. (See Mosiah 17:9-10.)

4. **Holy Ghost.** The Spirit was with Abinadi to the extent that he could withstand and confound Noah and his priests. The power in him was so strong that his face shone, and the guards feared to touch him. (See Mosiah 12:19; 13:2-6.)

5. **Jesus Christ.** Abinadi gave an excellent treatise on the mission of the Savior. (See Mosiah 13:27-35. Also see Mosiah 14-16.)

6. **Judgement.** King Noah and his priests purported to judge Abinadi and even God Himself. The irony is that it was Noah and his people who were on trial before God, with Abinadi as the witness. Because they refused to repent, the sentence was passed. (See Mosiah 11:27; 13:4; 17:7-8.)

7. **Martyrdom.** The blood of Abinadi stands as a testimony against Noah and his people. He sealed the truth of his words by giving up his life. (See Mosiah 17:9-10 and 20.)

8. **One, Importance of the.** It appears that there was only one believer of Abinadi's words. But, the succeeding record shows what a good and growing work came from the seed sown in Alma. (See Mosiah 17:2-4. Also see Story 24.)

9. **Peer pressure.** King Noah was just about to choose the right when his priests swayed him to take the evil path. (See Mosiah 17:11-12.)

10. **Power of God.** The power of God was manifested in Abinadi to the extent that his face shown and the people were afraid to touch him. He spoke with power and authority from God, withstanding and confounding the wicked leaders. (See Mosiah 13:2-7.)

11. **Pride.** Noah and his people were lifted up in pride. They thought, "How could we possibly be brought into bondage?" (See Mosiah 11:27; 12:15.)

12. **Prophecy.** Abinadi prophesied many things to these people, including their bondage and afflictions, King Noah's death, and the death of others by fire. As will be seen in the succeeding stories, the prophecies all came to pass. (See Mosiah 11:21-23; 12:2-8; 13:10; 17:15-19.)

13. **Prophets.** Though the record is silent on the subject, Abinadi, who lived amongst the people, must have gone through the requisite development to prepare him to become a prophet and a martyr. (See Mosiah 11:20; 13:26.)

14. **Sin.** The people had been taught to do evil. The wicked priests had studied, taught, and practiced sin for most of their lives. Iniquity was in their hearts; sin had become part of their beings. (See Mosiah 13:11 and 25-26.)

15. **Vanity.** At the moment when his conscience was touched, Noah's vanity dissuaded him from releasing Abinadi. (See Mosiah 17:11-12.)

* * *

STORY 24

ALMA ORGANIZES THE CHURCH IN THE WILDERNESS

Reference: Mosiah 17:1-4; 18:1-35; 19:1; 23:1-2

Background: *The sinful Nephites, ruled by wicked King Noah in the land of Nephi, were called to repentance by the prophet Abinadi. The people rejected the prophet's words and brought him before their wicked king, Noah. Abinadi testified before the King and his priests and then became a martyr by fire. (See Story 23.)*

Story Outline: Alma, one of Noah's priests, hears Abinadi testify in the court of King Noah. He believes the prophet's words and pleads with the King to spare Abinadi. But, Noah is more angered and orders Alma to be cast out and slain. Alma flees and hides himself. He writes down the words of Abinadi.

Alma repents of his sins and goes about teaching the words of Abinadi privately. Many believe him. He hides out in a thicket of trees near the waters of Mormon. Many believers of his words come there to hear his preaching and teaching.

On one occasion, when a goodly number are gathered together, Alma, begins baptizing his followers using authority from God.

About two hundred souls are baptized in the waters of Mormon. The converts call themselves the Church of Christ. Alma ordains lay priests to teach faith and repentance to the people. The church members meet at least weekly to worship God. They share their substance with the needy.

King Noah discovers Alma's movement. He claims that Alma is stirring up a rebellion and sends soldiers to destroy them. Alma and his people, about 450 in number, are warned of the army's coming and escape into the wilderness. The army does not find them.

Gospel Principles:

1. **Authority.** It is plainly pointed out that Alma acted by authority from God in baptizing converts and in ordaining other priests. (See Mosiah 18:13 and 17-18; Alma 5:3.)

2. **Baptism.** The requirements and covenants for baptism are set forth by Alma at the waters of Mormon. (See Mosiah 18:8-10.)

3. **Church organization.** The establishment of the Church in Alma's day was very similar to the restoration of the latter-day church. The Church was named. Membership by authoritative baptism was required. Priests were ordained and given stewardship for teaching and preaching. Doctrines were defined. Meetings were held for worship. A welfare system was put into place. Church members were to live together in love. The priests were to teach by the Spirit. (See Mosiah 18:17-29.)

4. **Conversion.** Alma was converted by the preaching of Abinadi. He in turn taught and converted others. On the one occasion, 204 people were baptized. The waters of Mormon were beautiful to those converts because it was there that they tasted of the sweetness of the gospel of Jesus Christ. (See Mosiah 17:2; 18:3, 6, 10-11, 16 and 30.)

5. **Covenants.** Baptism is a testimony or witness of the covenant we make with God to serve Him and keep His commandments. (See Mosiah 18:10 and 13.)

6. **Gospel of Jesus Christ.** Alma instructed the newly ordained priests to keep their preaching focused on the gospel: faith, repentance, and redemption through Christ. (See Mosiah 18:20-22.)

7. **Ministry.** The priests in the Church were not to be paid for their service, but were to earn their own livings. (See Mosiah 18:24 and 26.)

8. **One, Importance of the.** One young man amongst the priests of Noah listened to Abinadi's words with an open heart. From this one believer grew a sizable church of followers of God. Abinadi's martyrdom was not in vain; it bore fruit through Alma's conversion. (See Mosiah 17:2; 18:16 and 35.)

9. **Persecution.** As in the latter-day restoration, the organization of God's church was followed by persecution. Satan would like to destroy the Lord's work in its fragile infancy.

10. **Preaching.** The preaching was kept to the basic principles of faith, repentance, and redemption through Christ. (See Mosiah 18:7 and 20-22.)

11. **Records.** The people of Noah had not been taught the true gospel. Abinadi's words were revelatory to them. Alma was wise to write them while they were fresh on his mind. Thus, the teachings of Abinadi were preserved for the benefit of the church members and us. (See Mosiah 17:4.)

12. **Repentance.** Alma's life was changed by Abinadi's preaching. It was necessary for him to repent. He then dedicated himself to bringing others to repentance. (See Mosiah 18:1.)

13. **Teaching.** For the new church, much teaching was required: teaching the gospel to those who would hear, training the newly ordained priests, and teaching church members of their responsibilities. (See Mosiah 18:1-3, 7 and 18-29.)

* * *

STORY 25

WICKED KING NOAH
IS PUT TO DEATH

Reference: Mosiah 19:2-24

Background: *Noah was a wicked king who turned the Nephites in the land of Nephi towards evil. (See Story 22.) He put to death the prophet Abinadi who preached against his iniquities. Abinadi prophesied that his own death by fire would be a type of what should befall Noah. (See Story 23.) Alma, one of the priests of Noah, believed and taught the words of Abinadi in exile at the waters of Mormon. King Noah tried to destroy Alma and his followers who were formed into a church in the wilderness. (See Story 24.)*

Story Outline: Contentions amongst the people arise and opposition to the King breaks out. Gideon, in his wrath, pursues Noah to slay him. About to be overpowered, the King flees to the tower near the temple. From the tower he sees the Lamanites attacking and persuades Gideon to desist so that he can save his people.

The King leads his people in flight into the wilderness. The Lamanites pursue and overtake the Nephites. Noah commands the men to flee and leave their families behind. Those men who stay behind against the king's orders are spared because of the charm of their women before the Lamanites. The surrendered Nephites are taken, captive, back to their own land and are caused to pay half of their property to the Lamanites.

Gideon sends men into the wilderness in search of King Noah whom the Lamanites want delivered up to them. The party meets the men who had fled with Noah, now returning to the land of Nephi. However, the King and his priests are not with them. The men relate how they had repented and become desirous to return to their families. When Noah had commanded them not to go back, they had killed him by fire. The king's priests had escaped when threatened with the same fate. These men who had temporarily followed Noah return with Gideon to their families and submit to the Lamanite captivity with the other Nephites.

Gospel Principles:

1. **Choosing the right.** A moment of decision came when the King commanded the men to abandon their families. Some chose correctly, and others did not. (See v. 11-12.) Don't let the pressure of a situation push you into making a wrong choice.

2. **Courage.** Some of the men would not leave their families and flee with the King. They preferred to stay and perish with them. (See v. 12.)

3. **Parenthood.** Some of the men forgot their role as fathers to protect their families when they abandoned their wives and children. But later, they repented and realized their grave mistake. (See v. 12 and 19.)

4. **Prophecy.** Abinadi's prophecy that Noah's life would be as a garment in a furnace of fire was fulfilled. (See v. 20; Mosiah 12:3 and 10-12. Also, see Story 23.)

5. **Repentance.** The men realized that they had been led astray to leave their families behind. They repented and came back, no matter what the cost. (See v. 19 and 24.)

6. **Reward for wickedness.** The Nephite men finally became fed up with the king's wickedness and selfishness. Noah was put to death by his own subjects. (See v. 18-21.)

7. **Selfishness.**
    - King Noah cared more for himself than for his people. On the tower he lied to save his own life. (See v. 7-8.)
    - Again, to save his own life, Noah ordered his men to abandon their families. Self-preservation was his goal; it far overcame any concern for other people. (See v. 11.)

* * *

STORY 26

THE NEPHITES SUFFER
IN BONDAGE

<u>Reference</u>: Mosiah 19:25-29; 20:1-26; 21:1-18

<u>Background</u>: *Abinadi prophesied that unless the people in the land of Nephi repented, they would be brought into grievous bondage. (See Story 23.) In a surprise attack, the Lamanites came upon the Nephites, pursued them and made them captives in their own land. The wicked Nephite king, Noah, was put to death by his own men because he had commanded them to abandon their families during the attack. The men also sought to kill Noah's evil priests, but the priests escaped into the wilderness. (See Story 25.)*

<u>Story Outline</u>: Limhi succeeds his father, Noah, as king of the Nephites in the land of Nephi. He covenants with the King of the Lamanites to pay tribute of half of all that his people possess in return for a promise of safety. Limhi establishes his kingdom and has peace for two years. Lamanite guards are placed around the land.

The priests of Noah, in exile in the wilderness, kidnap twenty-four of the fair daughters of the Lamanites. The Lamanites think that the deed was done by Limhi's people and seek revenge. From the tower, Limhi discovers the movement of the Lamanite armies against him and prepares his people to receive them. A sore battle ensues in which the Lamanite king falls wounded and his armies are driven back.

The wounded Lamanite king is brought before Limhi where the cause of the attack is uncovered. Gideon deduces that the priests of Noah in the wilderness are to blame for kidnapping the Lamanite women. The Lamanite king is pacified toward Limhi's people and goes before the Nephites and convinces the Lamanite armies to retreat in peace.

The Lamanites keep their oath not to slay the Nephites, but they exercise unjust authority over them and afflict them with heavy burdens. The afflictions become unbearable. Three times the people of Limhi take up arms and attempt unsuccessfully to drive out the Lamanites. They are humbled by their defeats and cry unto God for deliverance. As the Lord had promised through Abinadi, He is slow to hear them. Yet, He does ease their burdens somewhat.

Gospel Principles:

1. **Communication.** If the King of the Lamanites had talked to Limhi about the kidnapping of the Lamanite women rather than jumping to conclusions and going to war, much bloodshed would have been prevented. Limhi also made no attempt at communicating before attacking. (See Mosiah 20:6-7, 9, 12-15 and 23-26.) In our personal relationships we often imitate the behavior of these two headstrong kings: we are ready to attack before talking out the problem.

2. **Humility.** It was only after a triple defeat that Limhi's people were sufficiently humble to realize that deliverance could only come from God. (See Mosiah 21:13-15.)

3. **Judging.** The Lamanites judged wrongly. The loss of many lives resulted. (See Mosiah 20:6, 14-15 and 23-24.)

4. **Prayer.** Even though the Lord was slow to hear their prayers, as Abinadi had prophesied, He did listen and answer in His own due time. (See Mosiah 21:14-16.)

5. **Prophecy.** In this story we see the literal and complete fulfilling of Abinadi's prophecies concerning these people. (See Mosiah 20:21; 21:1-4 and 15. Also, see Story 23.)

6. **Reward for wickedness.** Limhi's people brought upon themselves their captivity and afflictions by their own iniquities. Abinadi had been sent to warn them of the consequences of not repenting. (See Mosiah 21:5 and 12-15. Also, see Story 23.)

7. **Welfare.** Every man was commanded to impart of his substance to support the many fatherless families left by the battles. (See Mosiah 21:17-18.)

* * *

STORY 27

LIMHI DISCOVERS THE TWENTY-FOUR GOLD PLATES OF THE JAREDITES

Reference: Mosiah 21:25-28; 8:5-21

Background: *King Limhi and his people were in bondage to the Lamanites in the land of Nephi. They tried three times to free themselves by taking up arms against their enemies but were defeated soundly. (See Story 26.)*

Story Outline: King Limhi, desirous to find his brethren in Zarahemla, sends out a search party of men. They do not find Zarahemla, but instead discover a land full of bones and ruins from a destroyed civilization. Their supposition is that these are the remains of the people of Zarahemla. The men find twenty-four gold plates, which contain a record of this fallen people. The plates and other artifacts are brought back to King Limhi shortly before Ammon arrives from Zarahemla. (See Story 20.)

Limhi asks Ammon if he can interpret the plates so that the cause of the destruction can be known. Though Ammon cannot translate, he knows that King Mosiah in Zarahemla can. When Limhi learns that Mosiah has the gift from God to use the interpreters to translate ancient records, he is filled with joy. He gives thanks and praise to God.

This story completes the account of the people who left Zarahemla to find the land of Nephi that was given to Ammon to read. (See Story 20.)

Gospel Principles:

1. **Gifts of the Spirit.** Mosiah's ability to translate ancient records was a gift from God. Spiritual gifts are given to men to benefit others. The gifts are operated through faith by those who are commanded to use them. (See Mosiah 8:13-19.)

2. **Journals.** If the Jaredites had not kept a record on the twenty-four gold plates, we would know little of this entire nation. (See Ether 1:1-2.) Their bones and their ruined buildings give only an incomplete story. (See Mosiah 21:26-27; 8:12.) How complete is your personal history?

3. **Records.** King Limhi appreciated the importance of records. He presented the plates containing the history of his own people to Ammon to read. And, he was anxious to find someone to interpret the twenty-four gold plates because he knew they contained valuable information, lessons to be learned. (See Mosiah 8:5-6, 12 and 19.)

4. **Warning.** King Limhi was anxious to know the cause of the destruction of the nation whose bones were discovered. (See Mosiah 8:12-19.) Since we have *The Book of Mormon*, we can learn from the destruction of the Jaredites and the Nephites.

* * *

STORY 28

LIMHI'S PEOPLE ESCAPE FROM LAMANITE BONDAGE

Reference: Mosiah 21:29-36; 22:1-16; 25:4-9 and 14-18

Background: *King Limhi and his people were in bondage to the Lamanites in the land of Nephi. Their attempts to drive out their captors were unsuccessful. (See Story 26.) Limhi was overjoyed to be discovered by Ammon who came out of Zarahemla. The Nephites then had hope of deliverance. (See Story 20.) Ammon read the history of the people in the land of Nephi under the reigns of Zeniff, Noah, and Limhi. (See Stories 20-27.)*

Story Outline: Ammon and his brethren are sorrowed over the loss of lives, the wickedness of Noah and his priests, the martyrdom of Abinadi, and the departure of Alma and his people into the wilderness.

King Limhi and many of his people desire to be baptized, but no one in the land has the authority.

Ammon and Limhi and their people study how they can deliver themselves from their Lamanite captivity. Gideon proposes that the people evacuate through the back pass while the guards are drunk. An extra portion of wine is provided to the guards. Limhi's people depart by night into the wilderness, taking their provisions and precious things with them. They journey to Zarahemla where King Mosiah receives them and their records with joy. The Lamanites send an army out in pursuit. But, the army loses the tracks of the Nephites and becomes lost in the wilderness.

Mosiah gathers together all the people in Zarahemla. Included are Alma and his followers. (See Story 29.) The records of Zeniff and Alma are read to the people. Mosiah addresses them, then asks Alma to speak. Alma reminds Limhi's people that it was the Lord who delivered them. At their request, Limhi and his people are baptized by Alma.

Gospel Principles:

1. **Authority.** Limhi and his people wanted to be baptized. But, the ordinance could not be performed without one who had the authority and was worthy. (See Mosiah 21:33-35; 25:17-18.)

2. **Baptism.** Limhi and his people had repented and wanted to be baptized as a witness that they were willing to serve God. Their baptisms had to be postponed until Alma, who had the authority, could perform the ordinance. (See Mosiah 21:33-35; 25:17-18.)

3. **Compassion.** Upon hearing the history of the sojourn of Limhi's people in the land of Nephi, the people of Zarahemla felt joy for their joy and sorrow for their sorrow. (See Mosiah 21:29-31; 25:7-11.)

4. **Divine guidance.** Limhi and his people were reminded that the Lord provided their means of escape. (See Mosiah 25:16.) Too often, we take credit for the things the Lord has done for us, thinking that we did them alone.

5. **Goals.** The people were united in their goal to escape from bondage. Through their concentrated effort and the help of the Lord they achieved their goal. (See Mosiah 21:36.)

6. **Leadership.** Ammon and Limhi tapped into a great resource by involving the people to help solve their problem. (See Mosiah 22:1-2.)

7. **Redemption.** Limhi and his people had no way to deliver themselves from bondage. They thought they were all alone. When they realized that the people in Zarahemla existed, a means of escape appeared to them. Mankind was alone and without means of deliverance until Jesus Christ made His atonement to open the way for redemption.

* * *

STORY 29

ALMA AND HIS FOLLOWERS SOJOURN IN THE WILDERNESS

Reference: Mosiah 23:1-39; 24:1-25; 25:4-18

Background: *Alma was converted by the testimony of the prophet Abinadi in the court of the wicked King Noah. Alma was cast out and escaped his decreed death. (See Story 23.) Hiding in the wilderness, he taught the gospel privately, baptizing his Nephite followers in the waters of Mormon. King Noah sent an army after Alma and his people, who were then about 450 strong, but they escaped into the wilderness. (See Story 24.)*

Story Outline: The Lord strengthens Alma's followers so that the king's army does not overtake them. They settle and build a city in the land of Helam. Alma refuses the people's request to make him their king, pointing out the problems caused by the wicked King Noah.

A Lamanite army, which had been sent after Limhi's people and had become lost in the wilderness (see Story 28), comes into the borders of Helam. This same army had previously come upon Amulon and the other Nephite priests of King Noah in the land of Amulon. At that encounter, Amulon and his brethren had sent their Lamanite wives, whom they had kidnapped (see Story 26), before them to plead with the army for their lives. Because of the women, the Lamanites had shown compassion and had let the priests join with them.

In the land of Helam, Alma and his people ask the Lord to soften the hearts of the Lamanites to whom they surrender themselves. The Lamanites ask Alma directions to the land of Nephi, promising to grant him liberty in return. But, after Alma shows them the way, they go back on their promise. Lamanite guards are set round about the land of Helam. Amulon, who has worked his way into favor with the King of the Lamanites, is appointed king over Alma's people.

Amulon, remembering his former relationship as a priest of Noah with Alma (see Story 23), persecutes Alma and his followers. When the people cry to God for help, Amulon forbids prayer on threat of death. They continue to pray in their hearts. The Lord hears their silent prayers and makes their burdens light.

Alma's people keep exercising faith and patience until one day the Lord delivers them from bondage. All night they gather their possessions, and in the morning, they depart into the wilderness past their guards whom the Lord causes to remain in deep sleep. The escapees camp in the valley of Alma and give thanks to God.

King Mosiah receives Alma and his people with joy when they arrive in Zarahemla twelve days later. He gathers together all the people in Zarahemla and causes the records of Zeniff (see Story 28) and of Alma to be read publicly. The people react with joy and sorrow to the experiences that are related. The children of Amulon and the other priests of Noah, ashamed of their fathers, join with the Nephites. Alma teaches the joint citizens of Zarahemla many things and baptizes Limhi and his people. (See Story 28.)

Gospel Principles:

1. **Adversity.** The Lord sees fit to chasten and try us. If we turn to Him in our adversity, and trust in Him, He will support and deliver us. (See Mosiah 23:21-24; 24:10-14.)

2. **Authority.** As the High Priest, Alma held the keys of authority to consecrate other priests. (See Mosiah 23:16-17.)

3. **Bondage.** There is physical bondage, and there is slavery to sin. Alma's people were delivered from both types of bondage by the Lord. (See Mosiah 23:12-13; 24:13-16 and 21.)

4. **Compassion.** After hearing the accounts of Alma and Zeniff, the people of Zarahemla felt joy for their joy and sorrow for their sorrow. (See Mosiah 25:7-11.)

5. **Faith.** The faith of Alma's people was so great that the Lord was constrained to deliver them from bondage. (See Mosiah 24:16.)

6. **Gratitude.** Realizing that none but God could have delivered them, Alma and his people were full of gratitude. They gave praise and thanks unto Him. (See Mosiah 24:21-22.)

7. **Parenthood.** Amulon and the other wicked priests set such a bad example that their children turned away from them and adopted the name of Nephi. (See Mosiah 25:12.)

8. **Patience.** Knowing that the Lord was with them helped Alma's people exercise patience. (See Mosiah 24:15.)

9. **Prayer.** The prayers of Alma's people were heard and answered, even when outward prayer was forbidden. (See Mosiah 23:27-29; 24:10-13.)

10. **Repentance.** Before Alma could become an instrument in God's hands, it was necessary for him to repent. (See Mosiah 23:9-10.)

11. **Teaching.** An education that omits the teaching of the things of God is empty and incomplete. (See Mosiah 23:14; 24:1 and 5-6.)

12. **Trust in God.** Alma's people successfully passed the test. They trusted in the Lord and relied upon Him in patience and faith. (See Mosiah 23:21-24 and 27-29; 24:13-16.)

13. **Unrighteous dominion.** Amulon used his authority to persecute Alma and his people. (See Mosiah 24:8-9.)

* * *

STORY 30

ALMA ESTABLISHES
CHURCHES IN ZARAHEMLA

Reference: Mosiah 25:19-24; 26:1-39; 27:1-7

Background: *Alma and his people were welcomed to Zarahemla by King Mosiah after their sojourn in the wilderness. (See Story 29.) At a gathering of the people in Zarahemla, Mosiah called upon Alma to speak. Limhi and his brethren were baptized because of their faith on Alma's words. (See Story 28.) All the people in Zarahemla were united under the name of Nephites. (See Mosiah 25:13.)*

Story Outline: With King Mosiah's permission, Alma establishes churches throughout the land of Zarahemla, ordaining priests and teachers over each church. The seven churches are united in their faith in God.

Many in the rising generation, who were not old enough to understand King Benjamin's words (see Story 19), do not adopt the beliefs of their fathers. These youngsters refuse baptism and separate themselves from the Church.

Some church members commit sin and refuse to repent. The unrepentant ones are brought before Alma to be judged. Alma is troubled and asks King Mosiah to judge them. When the King refuses his request, Alma turns to the Lord. The Lord instructs Alma that only those who hear His voice are His sheep and shall be accepted into the Church. The names of unrepentant sinners are to be blotted out.

Alma judges the people according to the Lord's instructions. He and his fellow laborers regulate the affairs of the Church.

Those who are not members of the Church persecute the believers until King Mosiah proclaims that the persecution shall cease. Peace returns and the people prosper.

Gospel Principles:

1. **Church discipline.** The Lord provided for a weeding out from the Church of those who were unrepentant and rebellious. The names of those who would not hear his voice were blotted out. (See Mosiah 26:6-7, 21-22, 28-29 and 32-36.)

2. **Church government.** We follow the same principles of church government today that Alma did then:
   a) The Church has to have permission from the civil government to operate.
   b) The President of the Church holds the keys to ordaining church officers.
   c) The Church expands, opening new branches, as dictated by the sizes of the congregations.
   d) The doctrines issue from the President of the Church and are kept consistent throughout the branches.
   e) Repentance and baptism are prerequisites to church membership.
   f) The prophet writes the word of God.
   g) Judgement on church matters is conducted by church (not civil) officers.
   h) The names of those who refuse to repent are blotted out.
   i) Church leaders provide for their own support. (See Mosiah 25:19-23; 26:11-13 and 33-39; 27:5.)

3. **Generation gap.** Children's challenging the beliefs of their parents is not something invented in modern times. (See Mosiah 26:1-4.)

4. **Jesus Christ.** Those sheep who belong to the Good Shepherd will hear His voice and come into the fold of His church. (See Mosiah 26:20-24.)

5. **Persecution.** Contention between believers and non-believers is a universal problem. But, look how the people prospered when they put away their pride and haughtiness according to the command of King Mosiah. (See Mosiah 26:38; 27:1-7.)

6. **Prayer.** The reason that the rising generation did not believe was that they would not call upon God. (See Mosiah 26:4.)

* * *

STORY 31

ALMA THE YOUNGER AND THE SONS OF MOSIAH ARE CONVERTED

Reference: Mosiah 27:8-37; 28:1-9; Alma 36:5-27

Background: *Alma established and regulated seven churches in Zarahemla. Many in the rising generation were numbered with the unbelievers who refused to join the Church. (See Story 30.)*

Story Outline: Alma the younger, son of Alma, is a wicked and idolatrous man who influences people away from the Church into iniquity. He and the four sons of King Mosiah go about secretly to destroy the Church of God. An angel appears to them with power; his voice, like thunder, shakes the earth. In astonishment, Alma and the sons of Mosiah fall to the ground.

The angel chastises the young Alma for persecuting the Church. It is because of the prayers and faith of his father and the other church members that the angel came to him. After the angel departs, Alma is left so weak that he cannot move nor speak. He is carried to his father.

His father, recognizing the power of God at work, rejoices and calls for a multitude, including the priests, to be gathered together.

They fast and pray for Alma, the younger, for two days. Then, he stands up and confesses that he has repented "nigh unto death" and has become born of the Spirit.

From that time forth, Alma the younger and the sons of Mosiah travel throughout Zarahemla preaching, trying to repair the damage they have done to the Church. Mosiah's sons plead with their father, the King, to let them go to the land of Nephi to preach to the Lamanites. After consulting the Lord, Mosiah grants them their request.

Alma the younger remains in Zarahemla, where he becomes the first Chief Judge and the High Priest over the Church. (See Story 32.) Later, he recounts his conversion to his son, Helaman, describing his exquisite pain and torment, which gave way to exquisite joy and marvelous light as he repented and obtained forgiveness through the mercy and atonement of Christ.

Gospel Principles:

1. **Atonement.** The younger Alma remembered his father's prophecy about the atonement and called upon Jesus for mercy. (See Alma 36:17-19.)

2. **Conversion.** Though the mode of young Alma's conversion, appearance by an angel, is unusual, the result is common: a change of heart and missionary zeal. (See Mosiah 27:25-26 and 32-33; 28:1-4; Alma 36:22-25.)

3. **Faith.**
   - A father's faith that his son might be brought to know the truth was key to bringing an angel from heaven to visit Alma and the sons of Mosiah. (See Mosiah 27:14.)
   - As Alma the younger exercised faith in his father's prophecy about Christ's atonement for sins, he obtained mercy and forgiveness. (See Alma 36:17-19.)

4. **Fasting.** The extra power of fasting was added to prayer on behalf of the stricken Alma, the younger. (See Mosiah 27:22-23.)

5. **Forgiveness.** Alma the younger recounted to his son, Helaman, how he experienced sweet joy and marvelous light when his sins were forgiven through the merciful atonement of Jesus Christ. That joy was as exquisite as was his bitter pain during the repentance process. (See Alma 36:17-21.)

6. **Mercy.** The penitent Alma's plea for mercy was granted and he could remember his pains and sins no more. (See Alma 36:17-19.) The same mercy is available to all of God's children who repent and come unto Christ.

7. **Parenthood.**
   - The loving, prayerful concern of a father (and most certainly a mother, though the scriptures do not mention her) brought about a miraculous conversion of a son. (See Mosiah 27:14 and 19-20.) Mothers and fathers, do not underestimate the effect of your love and prayers on behalf of your children.
   - Perhaps the senior Alma thought that his preaching was falling on the deaf ears of his rebellious son. Yet, when the young Alma was in the gall of bitterness, encircled by the chains of death, he recalled his father's prophecy about Jesus Christ and His atonement for sins. This thought prompted the wayward son to call upon Jesus for mercy. (See Alma 36:17-18.)
   - Being concerned for the safety of his sons, King Mosiah consulted the Lord about the wisdom of letting them go on a dangerous mission to the Lamanites. (See Mosiah 28:5-8.)

8. **Power of God.** The ground shook under Alma and those with him because of the voice of the angel. (See Mosiah 27:18; Alma 36:6-7.) How much convincing of God's power does it take to bring us to obey His commandments? Can we have faith and obey without seeing an angel?

9. **Prayer.**
   - Here is proof of prayers being heard and answered:
     a) The angel was sent because of the prayers of faith.
     b) The young Alma's strength was restored through prayer and fasting.
     c) Mosiah obtained an answer to prayer concerning the safety of his sons.
     d) Alma the younger cried within his heart to Jesus for mercy when he was in the gall of bitterness and received forgiveness of his sins. (See Mosiah 27:14 and 22; 28:5-8; Alma 36:17-19.)
   - Today, our prayers on behalf of family members and ourselves cover the same subjects of spiritual and physical welfare.

10. **Repentance.**
    - Alma the younger repented "nigh unto death." He was given an understanding of the torment that the unrepentant ones will suffer. (See Mosiah 27:24-32; Alma 36:10-16.)
    - Alma and the sons of Mosiah sought to make restitution as part of their repentance. Not being able to bear the thought that any should perish, Mosiah's sons even went to their enemies, the Lamanites, to preach repentance. (See Mosiah 27:35; 28:1-4; Alma 36:24-25.)

11. **Reward for righteousness.** Though they had been the very vilest of sinners, the five young men were blessed because they repented and proclaimed the gospel. (See Mosiah 27:35-37; Alma 36:5-6 and 25-27.)

* * *

STORY 32

MOSIAH ENDS THE REIGN OF THE KINGS

Reference: Mosiah 28:10-20; 29:1-47

Background: *The four sons of King Mosiah and Alma the younger were converted by an angel that appeared to them as they went about the land of Zarahemla to destroy the Church of God. (See Story 31.) Subsequently, striving to undo the evil they had done, Mosiah's sons preached to the Nephites throughout Zarahemla, and then to the Lamanites in the land of Nephi. (See Story 39.)*

Story Outline: King Mosiah translates the twenty-four gold plates found by Limhi, which contain the record of the Jaredites. (See Story 27.) (The history of the Jaredites is treated in Stories 71 through 79.) Mosiah confers all of the records upon Alma, the younger, and charges him to keep and preserve them.

King Mosiah sends throughout the land to find out the will of the people who should succeed him. The people desire Aaron, one of Mosiah's sons, to be their king. But, none of his sons are willing to accept the kingdom; they prefer to preach the gospel. Therefore, Mosiah sends written word amongst the people pointing out the disadvantages of having a king. He suggests a system of judges chosen by the people.

The people accept Mosiah's recommendation and elect judges. They rejoice in their increased liberty. Alma the younger is made the first chief judge. He is also appointed by his father, Alma, to be the High Priest to govern the Church.

Gospel Principles:

1. **Freedom.**
   - Using the examples of King Benjamin and King Noah, Mosiah vividly contrasted the differences between the reigns of righteous and wicked kings. (Compare Mosiah 29:13-14 with Mosiah 29:18-20.)
   - The bounds of democracy are set by the Lord. (See Mosiah 29:25-27.)
   - Liberty (agency) carries with it individual responsibility. (See Mosiah 29:30-34.)
   - Given the chance, the people embraced their liberty and rejoiced in it. (See Mosiah 29:37-39.)

2. **Gifts of the Spirit.** The Lord prepared ahead the gift of interpretation by means of the seer stones for the benefit of those who should possess the land. (See Mosiah 28:13-16.)

3. **Knowledge.** The people were anxious to know about the Jaredites and rejoiced in the knowledge. (See Mosiah 28:11-12 and 17-19.) How will we use the knowledge that we have of the Jaredites and the Nephites?

4. **Leadership.** King Mosiah was an exemplary leader, and the people loved him for it. (See Mosiah 29:14-15 and 40.)

5. **Records.** The records were treasured and passed from generation to generation. (See Mosiah 28:11 and 20.)

* * *

STORY 33

THE CHURCH ENDURES TRIALS UNDER THE REIGN OF THE JUDGES

Reference: Mosiah 29:41-47; Alma 1:1-33

Background: *Alma the younger was appointed by his father to govern the Church as the High Priest. His father, Alma, who was responsible for organizing and regulating the Church in Zarahemla (see Story 30), died at age eighty-two. Mosiah, the last king, loved by his people, established laws and set up the government by judges before he died at age sixty-three. The younger Alma was elected by the voice of the Nephite people in Zarahemla to be their first chief judge. (See Story 32.)*

Story Outline: Nehor comes amongst the people in Zarahemla preaching false doctrines: that priests should be paid and that all people will have eternal life. When challenged by the faithful Gideon (see Story 28), Nehor, in his wrath, slays the older man with a sword.

The people bring Nehor to Alma to be judged. He is pronounced guilty of priestcraft and of shedding the blood of a righteous man. By the law, he is put to death.

In the second year of the reign of the judges, contentions develop between those who belong to the Church and those who do not. Pride leads to fist fights. The persecution is a trial of faith to the believers.

Some leave the Church. Those who remain steadfast stabilize the Church and are blessed. In their prosperity, the faithful church members are not lifted up in pride but remain liberal to all.

Exercising of the law against transgressors brings much peace amongst the people of Nephi.

Gospel Principles:

1. **Apostasy.** There were some church members who could not endure the trial of their faith under persecution. (See Alma 1:20-24.)

2. **Judgement.** The judgments of Alma were just. Priestcraft could not be allowed to destroy the whole nation. And, shedding the blood of righteous men could not be permitted. (See Alma 1:10-15.)

3. **Law.** The proper enforcement of the laws brought peace to the land. The laws were made by Mosiah and acknowledged by the people. (See Alma 1:1, 14, 17-18 and 32-33.)

4. **Ministry.** Contrast the pride and vanity of paid ministers to the humility and unpretentiousness of the lay priests. (See Alma 1:3, 5-6, 16 and 26.)

5. **Persecution.** There is a universal tendency for the world to persecute those who belong to the Church of God. (See Alma 1:17-19.)

6. **Pride.** Pride leads to downfall. Nehor's pride led him to murder and execution. The pride of some of the church members ended in their names being blotted out. (See Alma 1:5-6, 9 and 20-24.)

7. **Prosperity.** The Lord prospered the faithful members of the Church. They did not become lifted up in pride; they remembered the poor and were liberal to all. (See Alma 1:29-31.)

8. **Sin.** Beware! Hearing false doctrines and glamorous temptations too much can cause us to believe and embrace them. (See Alma 1:5.)

9. **Steadfastness.** Though the trials were difficult, the balance of the church members stood fast. The result was steadiness in the Church and blessings from the Lord. (See Alma 1:24-25 and 28-29.)

10. **Vanity.** There are always many who seek the vain things of the world. (See Alma 1:16 and 32.)

* * *

STORY 34

AMLICI SEEKS TO BE KING

Reference: Alma 2:1-38; 3:1-4 and 18-27

Background: *In the beginning of the reign of the judges in Zarahemla, the government and the Church faced some trials: Nehor's priestcraft and murder of faithful Gideon, and persecution of church members. Through enforcement of the law, peace was restored to the people. (See Story 33.)*

Story Outline: Amlici, a cunning man who follows the order of Nehor, gains favor with many people. His followers seek to make him king. Those who do not follow Amlici are concerned because he is a wicked man who wants to destroy the Church. The voice of the people is determined according to the law: Amlici is outvoted and rejected from becoming king.

Amlici is not content with the decision. He gathers his followers together, and they consecrate him to be their king. These Amlicites take up arms against their brethren to try to bring them under subjection.

Under Chief Judge Alma, the Nephites prepare for war. When the Amlicites attack, the Nephites gain advantage, drive them out, and pursue them. Alma's spies find out that the Amlicites have joined with the Lamanites and are heading to attack Zarahemla.

During their retreat to their home city, the Nephites are met by the much larger army of the Amlicites and Lamanites. The Nephites pray and are strengthened by the Lord. Alma slays Amlici. The Amlicites and Lamanites are slain in great number and are driven out into the wilderness.

Another attack by the Lamanites is repulsed by the armies sent out by Alma. Peace is again established.

Gospel Principles:

1. **Freedom.** The Nephites were justly concerned that Amlici would take away their religious freedom. They voted and later took up arms to defend that freedom. (See Alma 2:2-7.)

2. **Leadership.** Alma led his people as the High Priest and the Chief Judge. His active leadership is typified by him being right at the head of the armies with his captains. (See Alma 2:16.)

3. **Prayer.** It was because of the mighty prayers offered by the Nephites that they were delivered from the larger army of Amlicites and Lamanites. Similarly, Alma defeated Amlici because he was strengthened in answer to his prayer. (See Alma 2:27-31.)

4. **Preparation.** The Nephites acted upon their awareness of danger and armed themselves to prepare for the attack from the Amlicites. (See Alma 2:12-13 and 21.)

5. **Prophecy.** Prophecy is fulfilled whether or not the people that are affected are aware of the prophecy or of their role in its fulfillment. (See Alma 3:4 and 14-19.)

6. **Reward for righteousness.** We choose whom we will follow. We will be rewarded accordingly. (See Alma 3:26-27.)

7. **Reward for wickedness.** We bring upon ourselves our own condemnation. (See Alma 3:18-19 and 26-27.)

8. **Selfishness.** Amlici was not satisfied to go along with the majority rule. He still wanted to be made king. (See Alma 2:7-10.)

* * *

STORY 35

ALMA GIVES UP THE JUDGEMENT-SEAT TO PREACH REPENTANCE

Reference: Alma 4:1-20; 5:1-2 and 62

Background: *The first five years of the reign of the judges in Zarahemla were not without incident. There were contentions between church members and those who did not belong to the Church. (See Story 33.) And, there was a movement to overthrow the Nephite government that resulted in much bloodshed. (See Story 34.) Alma, the first chief judge and the High Priest of the Church, led his people through these trials.*

Story Outline: Within a period of three years, the people of Zarahemla change dramatically. The sixth year of the judges finds them suffering afflictions from their battles with the Amlicites. They are awakened to a remembrance of their duty to God. From the state of remembrance, the Nephites pass from peace and church growth to riches and pride.

By the eighth year of the judges, great contentions exist. The Church begins to fail. Alma sorrows because of the wickedness and inequality amongst the church members.

In the beginning of the ninth year, Alma gives up the judgement-seat to Nephihah so that he can preach the word of God, bearing down in pure testimony to tear down pride from amongst the people. Alma begins delivering the word of God in Zarahemla and then throughout all the land. He speaks by way of command to church members, and by way of invitation to those who do not belong to the Church.

The words that Alma preaches are recorded in Alma 5. His topics include:

    a) Being born of God, experiencing a mighty change of heart (see Alma 5:14),

    b) Being prepared for the judgement day (see Alma 5:21-22),

    c) Repenting from pride, envy, and persecuting (see Alma 5:27-35),

    d) Hearkening unto the voice of the Good Shepherd, not the voice of the Devil (see Alma 5:38-42),

    e) His testimony and how he gained it (see Alma 5:45-49).

Gospel Principles:

1. **Choosing the right.** Alma realized which of his two positions, chief judge and high priest, was the more important. He chose the better part. (See Alma 4:18-20.)

2. **Example.** The wickedness of the church members was a great stumbling block to the unbelievers who then went further astray. (See Alma 4:8-11.)

3. **Humility.** When times are hard, people are generally more humble. (See Alma 4:2-4.) But, even during the time when most of the church was lifted up in pride, there were some who were faithful, humble followers of Christ. (See Alma 4:12-14.)

4. **Pride.** Many of the church members set their hearts upon riches and took to wearing costly apparel. They looked down upon and persecuted others. Alma realized the destructive force of this

pride and sought to tear it out from amongst his people. (See Alma 4:6-10, 12 and 19.)

5. **Remembrance.** It took afflictions or powerful preaching to stir the people up in remembrance of their duty to God. (See Alma 4:2-4 and 19.)

6. **Riches.** Once riches came, pride followed. Though the rich had means to help others, they turned their backs on the needy. (See Alma 4:6-10 and 12.)

7. **Testimony.** Alma felt that the most powerful way he had to reclaim his people was to bear down in pure testimony against them. (See Alma 4:19.)

* * *

STORY 36

ALMA AND AMULEK
PREACH IN AMMONIHAH

<u>Reference</u>: Alma 8:6-32; 9:1-8, 23-25 and 29-34; 10:4-32; 11:46; 12:1-2; 13:31; 14:1-29; 15:1-2

<u>Background</u>: *Alma gave up the judgement-seat to concentrate on preaching the gospel to the Nephites in Zarahemla because they were lifted up in pride. (See Story 35.) After regulating the Church in the city of Zarahemla, he went to the city of Gideon where he found the church members in the paths of righteousness. (See Alma 6 and 7.) Alma returned home for a rest, and then, he went to the land of Melek. There he had much success baptizing the people. (See Alma 8:1-6.)*

<u>Story Outline</u>: Alma goes north to the city of Ammonihah to continue his preaching. The people of this city reject his words, revile him, and cast him out. On his way to another city, Alma is visited by an angel who commands him to return to Ammonihah and tell the people to repent or God will destroy them.

On his way back to the city, Alma is met by Amulek, who has been told by the angel, in a vision, to receive this holy prophet. Alma goes with Amulek to his house. Amulek feeds Alma. Alma blesses Amulek and tarries many days with him until both of them are constrained by the Spirit to go and preach.

When Alma begins preaching to the inhabitants of Ammonihah, he is again met with opposition. They ask who he is and who God is that Alma should prophesy that their mighty city would be destroyed in one day. The people are infuriated with him for telling them that they are lost and fallen. They seek to put him in prison, but the Lord does not allow it.

Amulek stands forth and preaches also. He introduces himself as a man of no small reputation amongst them and testifies how the angel told him to receive Alma as a holy man. Some are astonished at this second witness. But, the lawyers question Amulek to try to trap him. He sees through them and speaks against them. Zeezrom, one of the most expert lawyers, is confounded. (See Story 37.)

Alma begins to speak again. He establishes Amulek's testimony and preaches many things to encourage the people to repent. Many believe the words of Alma and Amulek. These believers begin to repent and search the scriptures.

Most of the people are angry; they bind the two men and take them before their chief judge. Witnesses are brought against Alma and Amulek. Zeezrom, now repentant, tries to defend them, but he is cast out with all those who believe in the words spoken by Alma and Amulek. Men are sent to cast stones at them, but Zeezrom escapes to the land of Sidom.

The wives and children of the believers are cast into the fire and burned up along with their holy scriptures. Alma and Amulek are forced to witness this martyrdom. They are constrained by the Spirit not to exercise the power of God to save the martyrs from the flames.

The judge, who is after the order of Nehor, strikes Alma and Amulek, questions them, imprisons them, and treats them harshly. For many days they suffer mutely without answering.

The judge and many of the lawyers and teachers visit the prison where Alma and Amulek are bound with cords. They all take turns smiting and taunting the two men. Then, the power of God comes upon Alma and Amulek. They break their cords. Their persecutors start to flee in fear. The earth shakes, and the prison walls fall, killing all but Alma and Amulek.

A few months later, the city of Ammonihah and all of its inhabitants are destroyed in one day in fulfillment of the prophecies of Alma and Amulek. (See Story 38.)

Gospel Principles:

1. **Angels, Ministering of.** It was to save the people from destruction that the angel was sent to Alma and Amulek with the message of repentance. (See Alma 9:25.)

2. **Blindness, Spiritual.** The people of Ammonihah had allowed Satan to get hold of their hearts. They could not understand nor believe Alma's and Amulek's words. (See Alma 8:9-13; 9:4-6; 10:24-25.) When we let Satan in, he will harden our hearts and blind us to the truth.

3. **Holy Ghost.** The Spirit was with these two missionaries in their ministry. They were given power of speech, guidance, and protection. (See Alma 8:10 and 29-32; 14:10-11.)

4. **Martyrdom.** Those who believed or had been taught the gospel were allowed to suffer death by fire to provide a witness against their evil persecutors. The martyrs were received up unto the Lord in glory. Their living executioners would have to face the wrath of God in their day of judgement. There are worse things than death. (See Alma 14:8-11.)

5. **Obedience.** After the angel told him to return to Ammonihah, Alma obeyed right away; he "returned speedily." (See Alma 8:18.)

6. **Power of God.** The Lord showed His power through Alma and Amulek, first in their preaching and then in their miraculous deliverance from prison. (See Alma 8:31-32; 14:26-28.)

7. **Prayer.** The prayers of the few righteous people were what prevented destruction of the land by the wrath of God. (See Alma 10:22-23.)

8. **Preaching.** Many believed the words of Alma and Amulek and began to repent. But, many more were offended by the plainness of the same words and sought to destroy the preachers. (See Alma 11:46; 14:1-2.)

9. **Reward for wickedness.** The Chief Judge of Ammonihah and his supporters were allowed to mock and punish Alma and Amulek for many days before they were destroyed. Their earthly destruction took place swiftly, but their eternal punishment was just beginning. (See Alma 14:14-27.) It often seems that the wicked go on, unpunished, persecuting the righteous. But, their day of judgement too will come, though not necessarily in this life.

10. **Sign seeking.** The Chief Judge of Ammonihah was very intent on seeking proof of the power of his two prisoners. When the sign was finally given, he and the others quickly recognized their impending doom. (See Alma 14:20-21 and 24-26.)

11. **Sorrow.** Alma suffered the sorrow of a missionary for those who would not hearken to the good news of the gospel. (See Alma 8:14.)

12. **Witnesses.** The testimonies of Alma and Amulek worked together. Each confirmed the truth of the other. (See Alma 10:10-12; 12:1.)

* * *

STORY 37

ZEEZROM IS CAUGHT IN HIS DECEIT AND REPENTS

Reference: Alma 10:27-32; 11:20-46; 12:1-11; 14:1-7; 15:1-12

Background: *After giving up the judgement-seat, Alma went throughout the land of Zarahemla preaching repentance. Guided by an angel, Alma teamed up with Amulek to preach to the people in Ammonihah. In this wicked city, the two preachers received much opposition, especially from the lawyers. (See Story 36.)*

Story Outline: Amulek accuses the unrighteous lawyers and judges of laying the foundation for destruction of the people of Ammonihah. The people cry out against him. Zeezrom, one of the most expert lawyers, skilled in the devices of the Devil, questions Amulek. Zeezrom tries to bribe Amulek with a large amount of money to deny God's existence.

Amulek catches Zeezrom in his deceit and preaches about the redemption and judgement. The people are astonished. Zeezrom begins to tremble under a consciousness of his guilt.

Then, Alma speaks to Zeezrom and the multitude. He exposes Zeezrom's effort as being a subtle plan of the Devil to ensnare the people with the chains of everlasting destruction. More convinced of the power of God, Zeezrom asks Alma to tell him more about the kingdom of God. Alma expounds upon the fall of Adam, physical and spiritual deaths, the atonement, the resurrection, repentance and redemption, and the priesthood. (See Alma 12:9-37; 13:1-31.)

In anger, the people bind Alma and Amulek, take them before their chief judge, and witness against them. Zeezrom sees that he has caused the blindness of the people and is pained with guilt. He pleads for Alma and Amulek but is reviled and cast out by the multitude.

Zeezrom escapes to the land of Sidom. There he falls sick with burning fever, tormented by guilt, and fearing that Alma and Amulek have been slain because of him. But the two holy men are actually delivered miraculously from prison. (See Story 36.) When Alma and Amulek come to Sidom, Zeezrom calls for them to come to him. He asks them to heal him. Through Zeezrom's faith in Christ he is healed and baptized by Alma. From then on, Zeezrom preaches truth to the people.

Gospel Principles:

1. **Conversion.** Zeezrom's conversion began when Amulek caught him in his deceitful lying. He became more and more convinced of the power of God by Alma's added witness. The consciousness of his guilt drove him to repent. His faith increased and he was baptized. (See Alma 12:1 and 7-8; 14:6-7; 15:4-12.)

2. **Deception.** Zeezrom sought to deceive Amulek and the people of Ammonihah. By so doing he was being a puppet in the hands of the father of deceit. (See Alma 11:22-25; 12:1 and 4-6.)

3. **Faith.** Alma was careful to question Zeezrom about his faith before calling upon the Lord to heal him. (See Alma 15:5-11.)

4. **Gifts of the Spirit.** Alma and Amulek were able to discern Zeezrom's thoughts through the spirit of prophecy. (See Alma 12:7.)

5. **Guilt.** Zeezrom, when convicted of his wickedness, felt guilt so keenly that he trembled. His burden of conscience became so great that it caused him to be sick with fever. The guilt was the trigger that started his repentance. (See Alma 12:1 and 7; 14:6-7; 15:3.)

6. **Integrity.** There was not even a question in Amulek's mind when tempted by Zeezrom. Of course he would not accept money to deny his testimony. (See Alma 11:22-23.)

7. **Preaching.** Many believed the words of Alma and Amulek and began to repent. But, many more were offended by the plainness of the same words and sought to destroy the preachers. (See Alma 14:1-3.)

8. **Repentance.**
    - Sometimes we, like Zeezrom, have to be caught in our sin before we will repent. (See Alma 12:1 and 7-8.)
    - Full of guilt, Zeezrom confessed before the multitude, trying to make amends. Because the people would not listen to him, he suffered greatly under poignant awareness of his guilt. Through the redemption of Christ he could repent and be healed. (See Alma 14:6-7; 15:3-12.)

9. **Riches.** Jesus taught that you cannot serve two masters. The lawyers in Ammonihah had definitely chosen to follow mammon rather than God. (See Alma 10:31-32; 11:20-23.)

* * *

STORY 38

THE CITY OF AMMONIHAH IS DESTROYED BY THE LAMANITES

Reference: Alma 15:15; 16:1-15 and 21; 25:1-3

Background: *The people of the city of Ammonihah rejected Alma and cast him out when he came to preach to them. An angel told Alma to return to Ammonihah to warn the people to repent or be destroyed. He met Amulek, whom the angel had also visited. The two men testified to the people that the city would be destroyed in one day if they did not repent. Those who believed the preaching were cast out, and their families were martyred by fire. (See Story 36.)*

Story Outline: About four months after Alma and Amulek are miraculously delivered from the Ammonihahite prison, Lamanite armies attack the city. All the people are killed and the great city of Ammonihah is completely destroyed in one day as prophesied. After the carcasses are mangled by wild beasts, they are piled up and covered. Because of the stench, the land is left desolate for many years. It is called the Desolation of Nehors.

During the attack, many of the Nephites from surrounding areas are taken captive into the wilderness. Zoram, Chief Captain of the Nephite armies, knowing that Alma has the spirit of prophecy, inquires of him where the Lord would have the armies go to find the captives. Alma asks the Lord and is able to tell Zoram where to meet the Lamanites.

Zoram and his two sons, with their armies, march into the wilderness and engage the Lamanites, scattering and driving them off. Every one of the captives is saved.

During the subsequent three years of peace, Alma, Amulek, and their helpers preach the word and establish the Church throughout the land.

Gospel Principles:

1. **Divine guidance.** Zoram and his sons stand out as faithful leaders who took advantage of guidance from the Lord. (See Alma 16:5-8.) All too often men ignore the divine channel of information.

2. **Faith.** If Zoram and his sons had not been men of faith they would not have considered asking Alma for guidance.

3. **Gifts of the Spirit.** Zoram and his sons went to Alma because he had the gift of prophecy. (See Alma 16:5.) Do we seek guidance from our spiritual leaders to take advantage of their gifts?

4. **Lost sheep.** Some useful steps to bringing back those who have strayed are demonstrated by Zoram:
    a) Desiring to reclaim the captives,
    b) Asking the Lord for guidance and help,
    c) Carrying out the Lord's directions to save the captives, and
    d) Setting them on their own when they are ready. (See Alma 16:4-8.)

5. **Opposition.** There are two conflicts depicted in this story, the one against the Lamanites and the one against Satan. (See Alma 16:8 and 21.)

6. **Prayer.** Amulek told the people of Ammonihah that only the prayers of the righteous people were keeping the city from destruction. (See Alma 10:22-23.) When the wicked ones cast out the believers and burned their families, Amulek's warning was ignored. (See Story 36.) The prophesied destruction followed shortly thereafter.

7. **Prophecy.** The destruction of Ammonihah was a direct fulfillment of prophecy. (See Story 36, and especially Alma 10:19-23.)

8. **Reward for wickedness.** The people of Ammonihah were warned of the destruction that would come if they did not repent. The Desolation of Nehors remained for years afterward as a monument and a reminder of their stubbornness.

* * *

STORY 39

ALMA HAS A GLAD REUNION WITH THE SONS OF MOSIAH

Reference: Alma 17:1-17; 27:16-20

Background: *After Alma the younger and the sons of Mosiah were stopped from persecuting the Church by an angel, they went about preaching the gospel to the Nephites, trying to repair the damage they had done. Alma stayed in Zarahemla and became the High Priest of the Church. The sons of King Mosiah went into the land of Nephi to preach to the Lamanites. (See Story 31.) The experiences of Alma during the first fourteen years of the reign of the judges are recounted in Stories 32 through 38.*

Story Outline: As Alma is journeying between cities, he meets the sons of Mosiah (Ammon, Aaron, Omner, and Himni) who are going toward the land of Zarahemla. For the last fourteen years, Mosiah's sons have been teaching the gospel to the Lamanites in the land of Nephi. Their reunion is one of great joy. In fact, Ammon is so overcome with joy that he falls to the earth, exhausted. Alma rejoices to see that his friends are strong in the faith. He conducts them to Zarahemla to his house.

The sons of the late King Mosiah report to the Chief Judge in Zarahemla of their joys and sufferings amongst the Lamanites: They

David S. Taylor

had left their father in the first year of the reign of the judges after refusing to have the kingdom conferred upon them. From Zarahemla they, with their party, had journeyed in the wilderness toward the land of Nephi. Much fasting and prayer was done along the way.

The Spirit of the Lord had told the sons of Mosiah to go forth in patience and long-suffering and that they would be instruments of salvation to many souls. Upon entering the borders of the land of the Lamanites, they had separated, each man going alone to declare the word of God to this degenerate people. Their experiences in the land of Nephi are given in Stories 40 through 43.

Gospel Principles:

1. **Brotherhood.** Alma and the sons of Mosiah were truly brothers in the Lord, drawn close to each other not only by shared past experiences, but, also by mutual growth in the common purpose of the gospel. (See Alma 17:3.)

2. **Courage.** It was a courageous mission that the sons of Mosiah undertook, going amongst the ferocious Lamanites. The fountain of their courage was the Spirit of the Lord. (See Alma 17:10-14.)

3. **Example.** The Lord told the sons of Mosiah to be patient in long-suffering to show the Lamanites a good example. Example is so important in proselyting. (See Alma 17:11.)

4. **Faith.** As they separated to go preach to the Lamanites, the sons of Mosiah were relying upon the Lord for protection, guidance, and success. (See Alma 17:13 and 17.)

5. **Fasting.** Through much prayer and fasting these missionaries drew close to the Lord. They received revelation, comfort, and power. (See Alma 17:3 and 9-10.)

6. **Friendship.** The friendship of these brethren was enhanced greatly by what they shared in the gospel. (See Alma 17:2-3; 27:16-19.)

7. **Joy.** The simple reunion of these friends after so many years brought joy. But, even more joy came from the knowledge that they were still brethren in the gospel, engaged in the Lord's work. (See Alma 17:2-3; 27:16-19.)

8. **Missionary work.** The sons of Mosiah were dedicated, exemplary missionaries. They served for fourteen years amongst the Lamanites. They prepared themselves through scripture study, faith, prayer, and fasting. Their preparation brought them the spiritual gifts of prophecy and revelation. They taught with power. Though they suffered many afflictions, they were blessed with much success. (See Alma 17:2-5.)

9. **Prayer.** Through much prayer and fasting these missionaries drew close to the Lord. They received revelation, comfort and power. (See Alma 17:3 and 9-10.)

10. **Scriptures.** Their diligent search of the scriptures made the sons of Mosiah men of sound understanding. (See Alma 17:2.)

11. **Teaching.** The sons of Mosiah prepared themselves to be effective teachers by searching the scriptures, praying, and fasting. (See Alma 17:2-4.)

* * *

STORY 40

KING LAMONI IS CONVERTED THROUGH AMMON'S EFFORTS

<u>Reference</u>: Alma 17:18-39; 18:1-43; 19:1-36

<u>Background</u>: *Ammon and the other sons of King Mosiah went into the land of Nephi to preach to the Lamanites. (See Story 31.) After fasting and praying for direction, the four brothers and those who were with them separated, each man going alone to declare the word of God. (See Story 39.)*

<u>Story Outline</u>: Ammon goes into the land of Ishmael. The Lamanites take him, bind him, and carry him before King Lamoni. The King asks Ammon if he wants to live amongst the Lamanites. Ammon answers, yes, and finds favor with Lamoni. He asks only to be a servant of the King.

Ammon is assigned with the other servants to watch over the king's flocks. At the watering place, some Lamanites scatter the animals. The other servants fear that the King will slay them for losing the flocks, as he has others in the past. Ammon sees an opportunity to win the hearts of his fellow servants. He comforts them and persuades them to gather back the flocks. They follow Ammon's instructions and bring the animals back to the watering place.

When the Lamanites stand to scatter the king's flocks again, Ammon places the servants around the flocks while he contends with the men, using his sling. He is protected from their stones and is given power by the Lord according to the promise made to his father, Mosiah. The men attack Ammon with clubs, but he smites off every arm that is lifted against him with his sword. Ammon drives the men off so that the king's flocks can be watered.

The other servants take the severed arms of the Lamanites before King Lamoni and explain what Ammon did. The King is astonished and thinks that Ammon is the Great Spirit. After Ammon is finished preparing the king's horses, he comes before Lamoni, but the King dares not speak to him for an hour.

Through the Spirit, Ammon perceives Lamoni's thoughts and explains who he is. Lamoni is more amazed because his thoughts are known. He promises Ammon anything he desires if he will tell by what power he does such marvelous works. Ammon's only desire is for the King to hearken unto his words. Lamoni commits to believe.

Ammon tells the King that the Great Spirit is God. He begins with the creation and expounds the scriptures concerning the fall and redemption of man. Ammon traces religious history down to the present time, including the rebellions of Laman and Lemuel. King Lamoni believes all of Ammon's words. The King cries to the Lord for mercy for himself and his people. Then he falls to the earth as if dead.

Lamoni is laid on a bed for two full days. His family mourns for him. His wife, the Queen, does not think he is dead and resists putting him in a sepulchre. Because her servants have told her that Ammon is a prophet with power, she sends for him and asks him to see her husband. Ammon, knowing that the King is carried away in God, is glad to fulfill the Queen's request. He tells her that Lamoni is not dead and that he will awaken on the morrow. She shows great faith and believes on Ammon's words, watching over her husband all night.

At the appointed time, Lamoni arises. He testifies to his wife that he has seen the Redeemer. They are both overcome by the

Spirit and sink down. Ammon and the servants of the King pray to God, the former in joy, the latter in fear. They are also overcome. The only one who remains standing is Abish, a Lamanite woman converted to the Lord years before through a vision her father had. She runs from house to house telling the people what has happened.

Disagreement arises amongst the multitude as they gather and see the King and Queen and their servants, along with Ammon, fallen to the earth as though dead. The gathered people think great evil has come upon the household. One man, whose brother was killed by Ammon at the watering place, lifts his sword to smite Ammon but is struck dead. Fear comes upon the multitude. Nevertheless, their contention over differences of opinion grows.

Sorrowed by the sharp contention, Abish takes the Queen's hand, whereupon she rises and praises Jesus. The Queen takes her husband's hand and he arises. Lamoni goes amongst the crowd teaching them the things Ammon taught him. Many are converted unto the Lord. But, many will not listen to the King.

Ammon and the servants of the King arise and go amongst the people telling of the miraculous things that they have witnessed. Many believe and are baptized. A church is established amongst these Lamanites who have turned to righteousness.

Gospel Principles:

1. **Attitude.** Compare Ammon's positive attitude with the negative and wasteful fear of his fellow servants when the king's flocks were scattered. Ammon saw the challenge as an opportunity, not a condemnation. (See Alma 17:28-31.)

2. **Blindness, Spiritual.** Though all witnessed the miraculous conversion of King Lamoni, many refused to listen to his words. (See Alma 19:31-32.)

3. **Conversion.**
   - It is very clear from this story that conversion comes by the power of the Holy Ghost. Missionaries can teach, but it is the Spirit that converts. (See Alma 18:40-42; 19:6, 12-13, 16-17 and 29-31.)
   - Conversion brings a change of heart such that people lose their desire to do evil. (See Alma 19:33-36.)

4. **Diligence.** King Lamoni was very impressed with Ammon's faithfulness in carrying out his orders. Ammon stuck to the task. (See Alma 17:31 and 39; 18:8-12.)

5. **Faith.**
   - Ammon was protected from death by the faith of his father, Mosiah, in the promise made to him by the Lord. (See Alma 17:29 and 35; 18:3; 19:23; Mosiah 28:7.)
   - The wife of King Lamoni demonstrated faith, even greater than that found amongst the Nephites. (See Alma 19:8-11 and 29-30.)

6. **Gifts of the Spirit.** Through the Spirit, Ammon was able to perceive the thoughts of King Lamoni. (See Alma 18:16-18.)

7. **Humility.** Ammon displayed his humility by asking to be King Lamoni's servant even though he was offered higher status. (See Alma 17:24-25; 18:17.)

8. **Leadership.** At the waters of Sebus, Ammon took charge of the situation. Though he was a newcomer and a foreigner, he emerged as the leader of the other servants. (See Alma 17:31-34.)

9. **Missionary work.**
   - Ammon was an exemplary missionary. He was humble, prayerful, and diligent. Guided by the Spirit, he was able to take full advantage of teaching moments. Ammon came to the Lamanites as a servant, not a master, and won his way

into their hearts through service. Then, with a little strategy, he put himself in a position where the King would believe his words. Ammon's good example gave him a reputation so that the Queen called on him for help. (See Alma 17:22-25 and 27-29; 18:8-10 and 16-23; 19:2-7.)

- Abish, though long silent about her belief, seized her opportunity to do some member missionary work. (See Alma 19:16-17.)

10. **Power of God.** Ammon was given power from God that he could not be slain. So great was this power that King Lamoni thought Ammon was the Great Spirit. (See Alma 17:35-38; 18:2 and 16-21.)

11. **Teaching.** Ammon's approach to teaching the King is instructive. He started with basic belief and understanding of the nature of God, probing Lamoni to find a common foundation to build upon. Then Ammon expounded the history of God's dealings with man, including the plan of redemption, from the beginning up to the present time. (See Alma 18:18-40.)

* * *

STORY 41

KING LAMONI'S FATHER IS CONVERTED

Reference: Alma 20:1-30; 21:14-23; 22:1-26; 23:1-5

Background: *Ammon, one of the sons of King Mosiah who went into the land of Nephi to preach to the Lamanites, brought about the conversion of King Lamoni in the land of Ishmael. Ammon became King Lamoni's servant, saved the king's flocks by showing forth the power of God, and then taught the King. Lamoni and his household were overcome and converted by the Spirit. Many Lamanites were baptized, and a church was established. (See Story 40.)*

Story Outline: King Lamoni wants Ammon to go with him to the land of Nephi to meet his father, the King of all the Lamanites. The voice of the Lord warns Ammon not to go, but rather to go to the land of Middoni to free his brothers from prison. Lamoni offers to come with Ammon to Middoni to assist by pleading with the king there.

On their way to Middoni, Lamoni and Ammon cross paths with Lamoni's father. When Lamoni explains to his father why he did not come to the feast and where and why he is going with Ammon, his father becomes angry and commands Lamoni to slay Ammon. When Lamoni refuses, his father raises his sword to slay his son. Ammon intervenes and, with his sword, wounds the old king.

Lamoni's father pleads for his own life. Ammon only asks the King to release his brothers from prison and to allow Lamoni free reign. Grateful to have his life spared and astonished at Ammon's love for his son, the old king grants these two requests. He desires Ammon and his brethren, when they are freed, to come visit him.

In Middoni, Lamoni finds favor with the king there, and Ammon's brothers are released from prison. Though ill-treated, they have been patient in their suffering. (See Story 42.)

Aaron and the other released prisoners continue to preach wherever they are led by the Spirit. Ammon returns with Lamoni to his home in the land of Ishmael where the King proclaims religious liberty and Ammon preaches the word of God. Lamoni's people give heed to Ammon's teachings and are zealous in keeping God's commandments.

Aaron is guided by the Spirit to the house of Lamoni's father, king over all the land. He finds the old king willing to listen and believe his words. Aaron expounds all things, beginning with the creation, including the fall of man and the plan of redemption. The King is willing to give up all of his possessions for the joy of eternal life.

Upon Aaron's instruction, the King repents and prays to God. He is struck as if dead. The Queen is called in by the servants. She is angry, thinking that her husband has been slain. She commands her servants to slay Aaron. When the servants refuse, in fear of Aaron's power, she sends them for reinforcements.

Aaron, wishing to avoid contention, takes the King by the hand and raises him up in the Queen's presence. The King ministers to his household and they are all converted. He pacifies the gathered multitude and has Aaron and his brethren preach unto them.

This newly converted king over all the land sends a proclamation to all of his people ordering them not to molest or persecute the sons of Mosiah. Thus, without obstruction, the word of God is preached throughout all the land amongst the Lamanites. Thousands are converted and churches are established with priests and teachers.

Gospel Principles:

1. **Anger.** The anger of Lamoni's father was so out of control that he was literally going to kill his own son. Ammon pointed out the consequences of such anger. (See Alma 20:13-18.)

2. **Conversion.** The cycle of the conversion of Lamoni's father follows a common pattern. At first, he was prejudiced against the people of God. (See Alma 20:10.) Ammon had to break down the barriers and get his attention. (See Alma 20:16-23.) The old king was astonished, and his curiosity was aroused by Ammon's words and example. (See Alma 20:24-27.) Curiosity led to desire, which progressed to faith, humility, and repentance. (See Alma 22:3 and 15-18.) The converted king helped to convert others and went on to become a defender of the faith. (See Alma 22:23; 23:1-5). Conversion had changed Lamoni's father from antagonistic skeptic to zealous believer.

3. **Divine guidance.** These faithful missionaries were directly led by the Spirit where they should go to accomplish the Lord's work. (See Alma 20:2-5; 22:1.)

4. **Example.** Lamoni's father was impressed enough by Ammon's behavior that he wanted to hear more about the gospel. (See Alma 20:26-27; 22:3.)

5. **Faith.** What an example of childlike faith we have in Lamoni's father! Here is the King over all the Lamanites, humble, teachable, and totally willing to believe Aaron's words. If only we could all pray with such simple faith as he did. (See Alma 22:7, 11 and 15-18.)

6. **Friendship.** The gospel tied Ammon and Lamoni strongly together in the bond of brotherhood. Their friendship so

impressed Lamoni's father that his desire to know more was kindled. (See Alma 20:4, 15, 17 and 24-27).

7. **Humility.** Lamoni's father demonstrated his humility as he knelt before the Lord, fully willing to give up all he possessed and all of his sins. (See Alma 22:15-18).

8. **Missionary work.** One can learn of missionary work by studying and applying the principles in the conversion cycle of Lamoni's father. (See Conversion, above.)

9. **Patience.** Aaron and his brethren remained patient even though they had to suffer all kinds of afflictions. The Lord remembered them and sent Ammon to free them from prison. (See Alma 20:2-5 and 29-30.)

10. **Prayer.** The first prayer of Lamoni's father was simple, humble, and full of faith. (See Alma 22:16-18.)

11. **Prejudice.** As is usually the case, prejudice melted away under the light of true knowledge when Lamoni's father found out what kind of person Ammon really was. (See Alma 20:8-10, 13-14 and 26-27.)

12. **Repentance.** Are you willing to give away all of your sins to know God? Is your desire the same as Lamoni's father's: to have the wicked spirit rooted out of your breast? (See Alma 22:15-18).

13. **Revelation.** King Lamoni was surprised that Ammon knew that his brothers were in prison, because the information came not by earthly means. We should so live that we can be prompted by the Spirit when needed. To those who are not spiritual by nature, knowing things by revelation will seem strange.

* * *

AARON PREACHES TO THE LAMANITES

<u>Reference</u>: Alma 21:1-17

<u>Background</u>: *After their miraculous conversion experience with Alma, the younger, the sons of King Mosiah, desiring to atone for their previous persecution of the Church, preached the gospel to the Lamanites in the land of Nephi. (See Story 31.) The four brothers separated to declare the word. After fourteen years, they had a glad reunion with Alma and recounted the story of their labors. (See Story 39.)*

<u>Story Outline</u>: When the sons of Mosiah and their party enter the borders of the land of Nephi, the brethren separate themselves to go forth amongst the Lamanites to preach the word of God. Aaron, one of the four sons, goes to the great city of Jerusalem, which was built by the Lamanites, Amalekites, and Amulonites. These latter two peoples, apostates from the Nephites, are even more hardened than the Lamanites. When Aaron preaches in the synagogues of Jerusalem, the people mock him and refuse to hear his words.

Aaron departs and joins some of his brethren in Ani-Anti where they find the people also hardened against the word. The missionaries move on together to the land of Middoni where they preach unto many, but few believe. Aaron and some of his brethren are imprisoned. After much suffering, they are rescued and released from prison by Aaron's brother, Ammon, and the converted Lamanite King Lamoni. (See Story 41.)

Aaron and his brethren go forth again, preaching wherever they can, as led by the Spirit. The Lord begins to bless them with success; many people repent and are converted.

Aaron is guided by the Spirit to the house of Lamoni's father, the King over all the land of the Lamanites. The King and his entire household are converted. Through the old king's support many doors are opened for these valiant missionaries, and thousands are brought to the knowledge of the Lord. (See Story 41.)

Gospel Principles:

1. **Diligence.** Aaron and his brethren did all they could to spread the gospel amongst the Lamanites. Imprisonment did not slow them down for long. (See v. 15-16.)

2. **Hardheartedness.**
    - Isn't it interesting that those who know the truth and fall away or rebel are more hardened than those who have never accepted it? (See Alma 24:30.) The Amalekites and Amulonites were former Nephites who had dissented. (See Alma 43:13.) They were more hardhearted than the Lamanites. (See Alma 21:3.)
    - The people in Jerusalem were so closedminded that they became angry, mocked Aaron, and refused to hear his words. (See v. 10-12.)

3. **Missionary work.** Aaron met with much resistance to his preaching. But, through sustained effort he was finally blessed with success.

4. **Persecution.** Those who embrace the gospel and would share it with others can expect persecution in some form. (See v. 10 and 13-14.)

* * *

STORY 43

THE ANTI-NEPHI-LEHIES BURY THEIR SWORDS

Reference: Alma 23:1-18; 24:1-30; 25:1-4; 26:1-37; 27:1-30

Background: *Through the efforts of the sons of Mosiah to preach the gospel in the land of Nephi, King Lamoni and his father, the King over all the land of the Lamanites, were converted. (See Stories 40 through 42.)*

Story Outline: The King over all the land orders all of the Lamanites not to persecute nor obstruct the sons of Mosiah and their brethren as they go forth preaching the word of God. These Nephite missionaries pass freely throughout the land and begin to have great success. Thousands of Lamanites are converted to the Lord. Churches with priests and teachers are established.

The Lamanite converts are so faithful that they never fall away. They lay down their weapons of war and stop contending with their brethren. These converts adopt the name of Anti-Nephi-Lehi to distinguish themselves from the Lamanites. They open correspondence with the Nephites and become an industrious people.

The hardhearted, unrepentant Amalekites and Amulonites, who are all dissenters from the Nephites, stir up the Lamanites against the people of God, the Anti-Nephi-Lehies. Preparations for war are begun.

The old Lamanite king confers the kingdom on his other son, the brother of Lamoni, whom he calls Anti-Nephi-Lehi. Then the old king dies. The sons of Mosiah meet in war council with the two brother kings, Anti-Nephi-Lehi and Lamoni. As led by their king, whose name they share, the Anti-Nephi-Lehies covenant to give up their own lives rather than shed the blood of man. They bury their weapons in the earth as a testimony that they will keep them bright and clean.

The Lamanites come against the Anti-Nephi-Lehies and slay 1,005 of them as they prostrate themselves in prayer before their attackers. When the Lamanites see that their brethren will neither fight nor run, but will praise God even in the act of dying, the slaughter stops. Over a thousand of the attackers repent and join the people of God.

Ammon rejoices over the success that he and his brethren have had amongst the Lamanites. Thousands have been converted through the power of God. Aaron accuses his brother of boasting, but he is only praising and glorifying the Lord.

Those Lamanites who are not converted divert their anger toward the Nephites and attack them in the land of Zarahemla. These angry Lamanites destroy the city of Ammonihah. (See Story 38.) After destroying Ammonihah, they find that they cannot prevail against other Nephite cities. They return to the land of Nephi and begin again to destroy the people of Anti-Nephi-Lehi who still will not take up arms.

After consulting with the King and asking the Lord, Ammon gathers the Anti-Nephi-Lehies and leads them into the land of Zarahemla to escape destruction. At the borders of Zarahemla, Ammon and his brothers meet up with Alma and have a joyful reunion. (See Story 39.) Alma escorts Ammon and his brethren to his home in Zarahemla and takes them to see the Chief Judge of the Nephites.

The Chief Judge polls his people and finds them willing to give the land of Jershon to the Anti-Nephi-Lehies and to protect them with Nephite armies.

The Anti-Nephi-Lehies take possession of the land of Jershon. They become known as the people of Ammon thereafter. They remain faithful, zealous members of the Church unto the end.

Gospel Principles:

1. **Apostasy.** The Amalekites and Amulonites demonstrated that those who turn away from the light become more hardened than those who have never sought it. (See Alma 24:29-30.)

2. **Commitment.** The people of Ammon made a strong commitment by burying their swords. We should confess and forsake our sins with the same dedication. (See Alma 24:17-18.) Announcing your intentions to someone else strengthens your commitment.

3. **Conversion.**
   • So complete was the conversion of the Anti-Nephi-Lehies that they never fell away. They remained firm, faithful, and zealous to the end. (See Alma 23:4-7; 27:27-30.)
   • What would normally appear to be a great tragedy, the slaughter of innocent people, turned into a blessing, in the eternal sense, with the conversion of more than a thousand Lamanites. (See Alma 24:23-27.)

4. **Courage.** What courage these converts had, to bury their swords and then go out to meet their attackers armed only with faith and prayer! (See Alma 24:15-16 and 19-22.)

5. **Divine guidance.** The King and Ammon relied upon the word of the Lord to guide them in deciding the destiny of the Anti-Nephi-Lehies. (See Alma 27:4-14.)

6. **Enduring.** It is remarkable that none of these converted Lamanites fell away. Their conversion was lasting. (See Alma 23:6-7; 27:27-30.)

7. **Example.** The hearts of many were touched by the faith of those who gave their lives rather than shed blood. (See Alma 24:23-27.)

8. **Faith.** Think how strong your faith in the atonement would have to be to lay down your life gladly without any attempt at defense. The Anti-Nephi-Lehies knew that if they were destroyed they would return to God and be saved. (See Alma 24:6, 15-16, 19 and 21-22; 27:27-30.)

9. **Forgiveness.** The Nephites were willing to give their former enemies a land for their inheritance and armed protection. (See Alma 27:21-24.) By contrast, the unrepentant Amalekites and Lamanites were trying to find someone to blame and take revenge upon. (See Alma 25:1; 27:2.)

10. **Hardheartedness.** Those who turn away from the truth become hardened against it as exemplified by the Amalekites and Amulonites. (See Alma 23:13-14; 24:29-30.)

11. **Missionary work.**
    - The proclamation of religious freedom in the land of Nephi opened the way for great missionary success amongst the Lamanites. (See Alma 23:1-5.)
    - Ammon well describes the joy that comes from missionary service. (See Alma 26:1-37.)

12. **Power of God.** Thousands of wayward Lamanites were permanently converted through God's power working miracles in men. (See Alma 23:5-6.)

13. **Repentance.** What a story of repentance of these Lamanites who considered themselves "the most lost of all mankind." They

became convinced of their sins, did all they could to repent, relied on the mercy of Christ, obtained forgiveness, received great joy, and committed never to murder again by burying their swords. (See Alma 24:9-13 and 23-26.)

14. **Reward for righteousness.** Ammon declared that he and his brethren had extreme cause for rejoicing in the fruit of their missionary labors amongst the Lamanites. (See Alma 26:35.)

15. **Reward for wickedness.** The city of Ammonihah was destroyed by the Lamanites because of the wickedness of its Nephite inhabitants. The people of Ammonihah had been warned by Alma and Amulek whom they had imprisoned. They had burned the wives and children of those who believed the word. (See Alma 25:2. Also, see Story 38.)

* * *

STORY 44

KORIHOR IS STRUCK DUMB

Reference: Alma 30:6-60

Background: *Ammon and his brethren, the sons of King Mosiah, brought thousands of the Lamanites in the land of Nephi to a knowledge of Christ. The faithful converts buried their swords, and many suffered death rather than return to their former murderous ways. The Nephites in the land of Zarahemla gave these people of Ammon an inheritance and protection in the land of Jershon. (See Story 43.) Meanwhile, during the fourteen-year mission of the sons of Mosiah, Alma the younger gave up the judgement-seat and retained his office as the High Priest over the Church in the land of Zarahemla.*

Story Outline: Korihor comes amongst the Nephites in the land of Zarahemla and preaches that there is no Christ. Many people are led into sin by believing his teachings. The people of Ammon, however, refuse to hear him and carry him out of the land of Jershon.

In the land of Gideon, Korihor is brought before the local high priest and the Chief Judge for questioning. Before them, he reviles against God and the priests and teachers of the Church. Because of the hardness of Korihor's heart they do not answer him but send him to Zarahemla to go before Alma and the Governor over all the land.

Korihor continues to blaspheme before the Governor. Alma, the High Priest over the Church, tries to reason with Korihor, but perceives that he is lying. Korihor asks for a sign that he may know that there is a God with power. Again, Alma tries to reason with him but to no avail. Korihor is given a sign by the power of God: he is struck dumb. By writing, Korihor acknowledges the power of God and confesses that he knew that God existed all along but was deceived by the Devil.

Korihor asks Alma to pray to God to remove his curse. Alma leaves it up to the Lord. But, the dumbness remains so that Korihor cannot lead the people astray again. He goes about from house to house begging for food.

The news of Korihor's plight spreads rapidly. Those people who had believed in his words are converted again unto the Lord. As Korihor goes about begging, he is trampled to death by the Zoramites.

Gospel Principles:

1. **Deception.** Satan deceived Korihor so that he went amongst the people spreading deception. (See v. 18, 42, 53 and 58.)

2. **Freedom.** In this story we see an interesting paradox. The laws of the land guaranteed Korihor his freedom of speech. Yet, he claimed that the Nephites were not free. And, all the while, he was the one who was enslaved, a puppet of the Devil. (See v. 7, 9, 12-13, 24, 42 and 52-53.)

3. **Gifts of the Spirit.** By the gift of discernment Alma knew that Korihor was lying. (See v. 42 and 52.)

4. **One, Importance of the.** The bad influence of one man, Korihor, could not be allowed to continue. The evil effect would be too great. (See v. 18 and 47.)

5. **Power of God.** Cursing as well as blessing can come from God's power. (See v. 49-50.)

6. **Reward for wickedness.** As vividly pointed out by Korihor's fate, the Devil does not support his children. (See v. 54-60.) Compare the Lord's promise. (See John 14:2-4.)

7. **Satan.** Notice the tools Satan used on Korihor and those who hearkened unto him: deceit, lying, carnal pleasure, and pride. (See v. 17-18, 42 and 53.)

8. **Temptation.** Those who were wise did not give ear to Korihor. (See v. 18-21.) It is only by heeding temptation that we become ensnared in sin.

9. **Worldliness.** Korihor's words (Satan's teachings) were pleasing to the carnal mind. (See v. 17 and 53.)

* * *

STORY 45

ALMA GOES ON A MISSION
TO THE ZORAMITES

Reference: Alma 31:1-38; 32:1-16; 33:1-2; 34:1; 35:1-14

Background: *The Zoramites, under the leadership of Zoram, had separated themselves from the Nephites. (See Alma 30:59.) They trampled Korihor, the Anti-Christ, to death. (See Story 44.)*

Story Outline: Alma, the High Priest over the Church, is sorrowed to hear of how the Zoramites are perverting the ways of the Lord. He takes several of his brethren with him to the land of Antionum to try to reclaim these apostates through preaching the word.

Alma and his brethren are astonished to see the Zoramites' mode of worship: They meet in synagogues once a week. One after another, each man stands on top of a holy stand called Rameumptom and offers the same prayer, thanking God that he is chosen of God and has not been led away by foolish traditions.

Alma is grieved at the hypocrisy of the Zoramites; their hearts are set upon riches and pride. He prays for comfort and success in reclaiming these people. Alma and those who came with him go off separately. The Lord provides for and strengthens them because of Alma's prayer of faith. The preachers begin to have success amongst the poor class of people.

As Alma is teaching on Onidah hill, he is approached by a multitude of people who have been cast out of the synagogues because of their poverty. He turns toward them, recognizing that they are penitent and prepared to hear the word. Alma tells them that they are blessed because they are humble. He then proceeds to give a discourse on faith, comparing the word unto a seed that grows in the heart. (See Alma 32:17-43.)

These poor people desire to know more. In Alma 33, Alma explains that the people do not have to go to the synagogue to worship God and that mercy comes through the Son of God. Amulek, in Alma 34, also teaches them, testifying of Christ and His infinite and eternal sacrifice. He also expounds on the subjects of prayer, charity, repentance, procrastination, and patience.

When they have finished preaching, Alma and his brethren go over to the land of Jershon. Meanwhile, the Zoramite rulers and priests find out those who are in favor of the words of Alma and cast them out of the land. These outcasts are received and nourished by the people of Ammon in the land of Jershon. The Zoramites are angered; they team up with the Lamanites and prepare for war against the people of Ammon and the Nephites.

Gospel Principles:

1. **Apostasy.** The Zoramites had fallen away from the true gospel by neglecting observance of church performances and daily prayer. (See Alma 31:8-11.)

2. **Compassion.** Look at the difference in how the cast-out poor were treated by the two peoples. The people of Ammon received the outcasts, nourished and clothed them, and gave them lands

for their inheritance. The Zoramites, on the other hand, cast them out, and were angry at the people of Ammon for receiving them. (See Alma 35:6-11.)

3. **Faith.**
   - Because of Alma's prayer of faith, the missionaries were provided for by the Lord. (See Alma 31:38.)
   - Alma gave us, here, one of the great discourses on faith and testimony, comparing the word to a seed planted in the heart. (See Alma 32:26-43.)

4. **Humility.** The people of Antionum were compelled to be humble and teachable by their poverty and social rejection. Alma pointed out that they were blessed by their humility, but more blessed are they who are humble without compulsion. (See Alma 32:2-6 and 12-16.)

5. **Missionary work.** The missionary experience is pretty much the same now as it was then. A missionary relies on the Lord, is provided for, exercises faith, has success with the humble people, and becomes an instrument in God's hands. (See Alma 31:34-38; 32:1-2; 35:14.)

6. **Prayer.**
   - A first step to apostasy is abandonment of daily prayer. (See Alma 31:10.)
   - Compare the prideful prayer of the Zoramites with the humble supplication of Alma. (See Alma 31:15-18 and 26-35.)

7. **Preaching.** Alma understood that the power of preaching is greater than the power of the sword. Effectual change to behavior must come from desire within the being, not from outside force. (See Alma 31:5.)

8. **Pride.** The Zoramites were blinded to the truth by their pride. (See Alma 31:17, 24-25 and 27-28.)

9. **Worldliness.** The more popular Zoramites did not want to give up their comfortable state; their consciences were salved by their once-a-week, perfunctory worship. (See Alma 31:23; 35:3.)

* * *

STORY 46

CAPTAIN MORONI STOPS THE LAMANITE INVASION BY STRATAGEM

Reference: Alma 43:3-54; 44:1-24; 45:1

Background: *Alma and his brethren went to preach to the Zoramites who were perverting the ways of the Lord. They had success in converting the poor people. However, the unrepentant, more popular Zoramites cast out their poor brethren and were angered when the people of Ammon received them in the land of Jershon. (See Story 45.)*

Story Outline: The Zoramites unite with the Lamanites and prepare for war against the people of Ammon and the Nephites. Zerahemnah, Chief Leader and Commander of the Lamanite army, appoints chief captains from amongst the dissenting Nephites (Amalekites, Zoramites, and descendants of the priests of Noah) because they are more wicked and murderous. The Lamanite armies assemble in the land of Antionum. Zerahemnah's design is to stir up his people to anger against the Nephites so that he can gain more power.

In the land of Jershon, the Nephite armies, led by Chief Captain Moroni (only twenty-five years old), prepare to meet the Lamanites. The design of the Nephites is to protect and preserve their lands, people, and liberty. The Nephites are also committed to protect the people of Ammon, the converted Lamanites who have vowed never again to take up arms. (See Story 43.)

Upon their attack, the scantily-clad Lamanites are frightened away because Moroni has protected his soldiers with shields and armor. The Lamanite attackers retreat into the wilderness and plan to strike the land of Manti instead of Jershon. Moroni learns of their plans by using spies, which he considers to be a justifiable stratagem, and by asking Alma to inquire of the Lord.

The armies of Moroni ambush the Lamanites as they begin to cross the river Sidon into the land of Manti. The fighting is fierce, but by calling upon God, the Nephites gain the advantage. They surround the Lamanites and offer to cease killing them if they will lay down their arms and covenant not to attack the Nephites again. Zerahemnah offers to lay down his arms but will not take an oath. Moroni remains steadfast in his demands.

Zerahemnah rushes against Moroni but is stopped and scalped by one of Moroni's soldiers. Many Lamanites see their Chief's scalp hoisted forth on the tip of the soldier's sword and lay down their arms with an oath of peace. But, Zerahemnah, in his wrath, stirs up the rest of his soldiers to fight powerfully. Moroni and his army fall upon the Lamanites and slay them until Zerahemnah is compelled to surrender and take the oath.

After disposing of the numerous dead, the Nephites return to their homes rejoicing that the Lord has delivered them.

Gospel Principles:

1. **Apostasy.** Those who once embraced the gospel, when they turn against it, can easily become bitter and more wicked than those who never knew the Lord. (See Alma 43:6 and 13.)

2. **Faith.** In leading his army, Moroni had faith to ask for the Lord's guidance through the prophet Alma. And, Moroni recognized the Lord's hand in giving the Nephites victory. (See Alma 43:23; 44:3-4.)

3. **Gratitude.** The Nephites remembered to thank the Lord for delivering them from their enemies. (See Alma 45:1.)

4. **Integrity.** An oath meant something in those days. Moroni was confident enough to let the Lamanites go free if they vowed never again to attack the Nephites. (See Alma 44:6-8, 15 and 19.)

5. **Mercy.** Moroni was merciful in giving the Lamanites a chance to surrender and save their lives. (See Alma 43:53-54; 44:1.)

6. **Persecution.** The Lamanites hated the Nephites for their belief in God. (See Alma 43:11; 44:2.)

7. **Prayer.** The unified prayers of the Nephite soldiers turned the tide at the height of the battle. (See Alma 43:49-50.)

8. **Preparation.** Moroni had so prepared his soldiers with armor and weapons that the Lamanites were afraid to attack them. (See Alma 43:4 and 17-22.)

9. **Prophets.** Moroni's military success was due largely to his willingness to consult and give heed to the prophet. (See Alma 43:23-24.)

10. **Youth.** Moroni was only twenty-five years old when he was put in command of all the Nephite armies. A great man all of his life, he distinguished himself early. (See Alma 43:16-17; 48:17.)

* * *

STORY 47

CAPTAIN MORONI RAISES THE TITLE OF LIBERTY

<u>Reference</u>: Alma 45:20-24; 46:1-37

<u>Background</u>: *Under Chief Captain Moroni, the Nephite armies stopped the Lamanite attack led by Zerahemnah. The surrendering Lamanite soldiers were forced to take an oath of peace. The Nephites rejoiced and gave thanks unto the Lord for their deliverance. They fasted and prayed much and worshiped God joyfully. (See Story 46.) After prophesying of the final destruction of the Nephites and blessing his sons and the Church, Alma, the High Priest over the Church, departed never to be heard of again. (See Alma 45:9-19.)*

<u>Story Outline</u>: Alma's oldest son, Helaman, and his brethren, high priests over the Church (see Alma 46:6), go throughout all the land appointing priests and teachers to regulate the Church. Because of riches and pride, many people refuse to give heed to the word of God. Led by Amalickiah, who seeks to be king, these people gather together against Helaman and his brethren. Amalickiah's flattering words and promises of power to his supporters lead away the hearts of many of the people, including church members.

Captain Moroni is angry with Amalickiah because of the dissensions. He writes a patriotic phrase on a piece of his coat and fastens it to the end of a pole, calling it the title of liberty. In mighty prayer, he asks for the Lord's blessings upon the followers of Christ, that their freedom might be preserved.

Waving the title of liberty, Moroni goes amongst the people calling them to covenant with God to maintain their rights and religion. People gather to him, girded in armor. They rend their garments as a token of their covenant.

Throughout all the land, those who will stand for liberty are gathered by Moroni. When Amalickiah realizes that his followers are outnumbered, he takes as many as will follow him and departs into the Lamanite land of Nephi. Moroni, realizing that these dissenters would add strength to their enemies, the Lamanites, pursues the Amalickiahites with his army to cut them off. Though Amalickiah and a few of his men escape, most are captured and taken back to Zarahemla. Those who will not take the oath to support freedom are put to death. (Those who refuse the covenant of freedom are few.)

Gospel Principles:

1. **Church organization.** The high priests appointed priests and teachers in all the churches to take care of and regulate the Church. (See Alma 45:22; 46:6.)

2. **Contention.** The dissensions amongst the people were not quelled by the preaching of the word of God, rather, the division increased. (See Alma 45:21-24.)

3. **Forgetfulness.** How quickly the people turned away from Him who had delivered and blessed them. (See Alma 46:7-8.)

4. **Freedom.** Would the story have been different if Moroni had not acted boldly to rally the people to preserve their freedom? If apathy had prevailed, their freedom would probably have been lost. (See Alma 46:11-22.)

5. **Leadership.** What a leader Moroni was! He prayed for help, raised a standard, and rallied the righteous people throughout the whole land. He followed through and raised the title of liberty on all the towers to remind the people. (See Alma 46:16-22, 28 and 34-36.)

6. **One, Importance of the.** One man, whether wicked like Amalickiah or righteous like Moroni, can have great influence over a group of people. (See Alma 46:9-10 and 21-22.)

7. **Patriotism.** The title of liberty gave the people a standard to rally behind, to remind them of their heritage. (See Alma 46:12 and 19-21.)

8. **Pride.** Riches led to pride, which made the people easy prey for Amalickiah's flattery. (See Alma 45:23-24; 46:5-7.)

9. **Repentance.** Moroni attempted to stop all of the followers of Amalickiah so that they would not add strength to the enemy, but a small group escaped. Just like sin that is not completely rooted out, we will see in future stories that Amalickiah will come back to cause more trouble. (See Alma 46:30-33.)

10. **Riches.** In the dissenters' own eyes, their riches made themselves better than others, so much better that they thought they were above the word of God preached by the church leaders. Beware of riches. (See Alma 45:23-24.)

* * *

STORY 48

AMALICKIAH BECOMES
KING BY TREACHERY

Reference: Alma 47:1-36; 48:1-25; 49:1-30; 50:1-24

Background: *Amalickiah sought to be king of the Nephites. His flattery bought him supporters until Captain Moroni rallied the people to preserve their freedom. Amalickiah was thwarted but he escaped with a few followers to the Lamanites in the land of Nephi. (See Story 47.)*

Story Outline: Amalickiah stirs up the Lamanites to anger against the Nephites to the point that the Lamanite king orders his people to gather for war. When many refuse the call to war, the King charges Amalickiah to lead the army of the obedient soldiers to compel the others to follow.

Amalickiah's plan is to take over as king of the Lamanites. He already has the favor of those who obey the present king. He betrays the army he is leading and gives them into the hands of Lehonti, the leader of the dissenting army: Amalickiah allows Lehonti's men to surround his army while they sleep. In return, Amalickiah asks to be second in command to Lehonti. When Amalickiah's men awaken and find that they are surrounded, they plead with Amalickiah to let them join in with their brethren. The two armies combine, with Amalickiah placed second in command, just as he had planned.

By secretly administering poison to Lehonti, Amalickiah secures his desired position as chief commander of the joint Lamanite army. He marches the army back to the city of Nephi. When the King of the Lamanites comes out to meet them, Amalickiah causes his servant to stab the King. The king's servants flee. Amalickiah blames the fleeing servants for the king's death and has his army pursue them. Thus, by fraud, he gains the favor of the people and deceives the Queen as to her husband's death. He achieves his original goal by marrying the Queen and becoming king of the Lamanites.

Still not satisfied, Amalickiah plans to bring the Nephites into bondage so that he can rule over the entire land. He stirs up the Lamanites to anger against the Nephites and gathers a large army.

Meanwhile, Moroni is encouraging the Nephites to obey God and prepare fortifications to protect their liberty. The Nephites live together in peace for four years without internal strife.

The Lamanite armies march on the partially rebuilt Nephite city of Ammonihah. But, they are surprised to find this former weak spot strengthened and fortified with a dirt ridge. They dare not attack even though they have armor and outnumber the Nephites.

A retreat and an approach on the city of Noah follow. Whereas the city of Noah was formerly the weakest place, it is now stronger and better fortified than the city of Ammonihah. Though the Lamanites fear Lehi, who commands the Nephites in the city of Noah, they must attack because of an oath that their leaders have sworn. The Nephites are all but invincible behind their earthen forts. They experience no casualties while slaying more than a thousand Lamanites, including all of their chief captains. King Amalickiah is furious about not bringing the Nephites into bondage and swears to drink Moroni's blood.

The Nephites thank the Lord for His protection. Under Moroni's direction they continue to prepare their defenses, building forts of earth and timbers around every city. The Lamanites are driven out of the east wilderness. The line between the Nephites on the north (land of Zarahemla) and the Lamanites on the south (land of Nephi) is fortified from west to east. New Nephite cities are built. The Nephites are prosperous and happy.

Gospel Principles:

1. **Apostasy.** The apostate Nephites became worse than the Lamanites. (See Alma 47:35-36.)

2. **Character.** What a man was this Moroni, a wonderful example of integrity for us to follow. He was strong, true, fair, faithful, firm, dedicated to service, and full of understanding. (See Alma 48:11-13 and 16-19.)

3. **Deception.** Lies, conspiracy, and murder were the tools of Amalickiah, a master deceiver. He was so cunning that he not only gained the throne but turned the hearts of the Lamanites totally. The large portion of the people who initially refused to go to war against the Nephites were martialed into going to war after all. (See Alma 47:4, 8, 13-19, 22-30 and 33-35; 48:1-3)

4. **Faith.** The Nephites had faith that the Lord would protect and prosper them if they kept His commandments. (See Alma 48:15-16.)

5. **Gratitude.** Moroni and his people were grateful to God for their blessings. Compare Amalickiah's attitude. (See Alma 48:12; 49:27-28.)

6. **Greed.** It was not enough for Amalickiah to be king over all of the Lamanites. He also wanted all of the Nephites under his rule. (See Alma 48:2-4.)

7. **Happiness.** The Nephites were blessed with peace and prosperity because they kept the commandments. "There never was a happier time amongst the people of Nephi." (See Alma 49:30; 50:17-23.)

8. **Leadership.** Contrast the two leaders in this story. Moroni, full of faith and gratitude, sought diligently for the liberty and welfare of his people. Amalickiah, greedy and deceitful, was out for his own personal gain. (See Alma 48:7-18; 49:26-28.)

9. **Preparation.** Moroni was a master strategist. Under his leadership the Nephites were prepared spiritually and physically. We too should prepare to meet the adversary by strengthening our weaknesses. We can also learn from Moroni about being prepared for possible future physical calamities. (See Alma 48:7-10, 14-16 and 22-25; 49:2-9 and 13-20; 50:1-6.)

10. **Weakness.** This story gives us a key for resisting and overcoming temptations. Realize what your weak places are and use strategy to strengthen them and protect yourself. (See Alma 48:9; 49:14.)

* * *

STORY 49

THE PEOPLE OF MORIANTON REBEL OVER A LAND CLAIM

Reference: Alma 50:23-36

Background: *In the days of Captain Moroni, the people of Nephi enjoyed a prosperous and happy three years. The attacking Lamanites, commanded by King Amalickiah, were repulsed, and Moroni further prepared the defenses of his people. (See Story 48.)*

Story Outline: A dispute arises amongst the Nephites over land boundaries. Morianton and his people claim a part of the land of Lehi. The contention warms to the point that the people of Morianton take up arms against their brethren.

The people of Lehi flee to Moroni's camp for assistance. Morianton, fearing Moroni's retribution, flees northward with his people. He beats one of his maid servants who escapes and tells Moroni of the escape plan.

To stop the threat of future loss of liberty, Moroni sends an army, under Teancum, to head the people of Morianton. Due to the stubbornness of the fleeing group and their wicked leader, a battle ensues. Teancum slays Morianton. The rebels are brought back as prisoners. Upon covenanting to keep the peace, the captives are restored to their lands and freedom.

Gospel Principles:

1. **Choosing the right.** Morianton and his people knew they were in the wrong. They could have repented but chose to flee. (See v. 28-29.)

2. **Forgiveness.** We do not read of punishment or grudges here. The errant ones were simply restored to their lands upon covenanting to keep the peace. (See v. 36.)

3. **Greed.** The seed that gave rise to the contention in this story was greed: desire for more land. (See v. 26.)

4. **Stubbornness.** Had it not been for stubbornness, the armed conflict could have been avoided. (See v. 35.)

5. **Unrighteous dominion.** Misguided by flattering words, the people of Morianton were swayed into taking the wrong course. History is full of examples of faithful followers led astray by unrighteous dictators. (See v. 29 and 35.)

* * *

STORY 50

NEPHITE KING-MEN WEAKEN THEIR NATION'S DEFENSE

Reference: Alma 50:37-40; 51:1-37; 52:1-40; 53:1-7

Background: *Peace was restored to the Nephites after Captain Moroni stopped the dissension of the people of Morianton. (See Story 49.) Nephihah served as the second chief judge over the people. (See Story 35.)*

Story Outline: Pahoran is appointed to be the Chief Judge in the land of Zarahemla upon the death of his father, Nephihah. Part of the people wants the laws changed back to government by a king. Pahoran refuses to change the law and incurs the anger of this group that call themselves king-men. The dispute heats up as the king-men seek to impeach the Chief Judge, while the freemen support him in maintaining a free government. By a vote of the people, Pahoran keeps his position in the judgement-seat.

During this period of internal strife, Amalickiah, the Nephite traitor who became king of the Lamanites and has vowed to drink Moroni's blood (see Story 48), builds up his army, preparing to attack the Nephites.

The Nephite king-men, angered by the Chief Judge and the freemen, refuse to take up arms to defend their country. Moroni is very angry. Realizing the need to put down the internal rebellion to be strong against the external foe, he obtains permission to compel the king-men to take up arms upon penalty of death. Four thousand dissenters are hewn down by his army. The surviving leaders are imprisoned. The rest of the rebels agree to take up the standard of liberty and bear arms to defend their country.

Meanwhile, the Lamanite army, under the command of Amalickiah, advances, taking several cities on the east border by the seashore. He and his army are met and stopped by Teancum's strong and skillful Nephite warriors. Teancum sneaks into the Lamanite camp at night and slays Amalickiah.

Amalickiah's brother, Ammoron, is appointed as the new king of the Lamanites. He gathers another army and attacks the Nephites on the western border while his armies on the eastern shore hold the cities they have taken. Moroni is engaged in the west and delays joining and strengthening Teancum in the east.

When Moroni is finally able to join Teancum, he devises a plan for decoying the Lamanites out of their strongholds in the city of Mulek. The Lamanites are drawn out to pursue Teancum with his small, decoy army. Teancum heads toward the city of Bountiful from whence Lehi, with a Nephite army, comes out against the Lamanites. Meanwhile, Moroni takes the city of Mulek and follows in the rear after the Lamanites. As the march-weary Lamanites retreat from Lehi's fresh forces, they are met by Moroni's army. A fierce battle ensues with the Lamanites trapped between the two Nephite armies. Finally, most of the Lamanites surrender their weapons.

Moroni uses the numerous Lamanite prisoners to bury the dead and then to fortify the city of Bountiful with a ditch and strong wall of earth and timbers round about it. The Nephites make more preparations for war under Moroni's direction.

<u>Gospel Principles:</u>

1. **Grudge holding.** The oath to drink Moroni's blood that Amalickiah made brought about his downfall. (See Alma 51:9-10 and 27-34.)

2. **Law.** There is a proper way to change laws. Rebelling, as the king-men did, is not the proper way. They were not willing to live by the voice of the people in obeying the laws of the land. (See Alma 51:2-7 and 13.)

3. **Preparation.** Moroni was ever a man of preparation. He realized that the internal dissension had to be rooted out to allow for a strong external defense. Even so, we must purify our inner vessels so that we will be better prepared to serve others. (See Alma 51:9, 13 and 22-23; 53:7; Luke 22:31-32.)

4. **Pride.** It was the pride of the supposedly highborn king-men that weakened the Nephite nation during this crucial time. (See Alma 51:8, 17 and 21.)

5. **Temptation.** The Lamanites were tempted out of their stronghold by a decoy. Satan will show us enticing sins to tempt us away from our strength so that he can take possession of our houses. (See Alma 52:22-26.)

6. **Unrighteous dominion.** The goal of the king-men was to have power and authority over the people. (See Alma 51:8.)

* * *

STORY 51

HELAMAN'S TWO THOUSAND STRIPLING WARRIORS ARE PRESERVED BY FAITH

Reference: Alma 53:8-22; 56:1-57; 57:6 and 19-27; 58:39-40

Background: *The Lamanites attacked the Nephites on the east and west borders. Teancum led the Nephite armies in the east. After putting things right in the west, Captain Moroni, with his army, joined and strengthened Teancum in the east. Together, using strategy, Teancum and Moroni decoyed the Lamanites and took back the city of Mulek. (See Story 50.)*

Thousands of Lamanites in the land of Nephi were converted to the Lord through the missionary efforts of Ammon and the other sons of Mosiah. These converts buried their weapons of war with an oath never more to shed blood. First known as the Anti-Nephi-Lehies and later as the people of Ammon or Ammonites, these faithful people chose to perish at the hands of their unconverted brethren rather than break their oath. To prevent their further destruction, Ammon appealed to the Nephites who consented to provide them an inheritance and protection in the land of Jershon. (See Story 43.)

Story Outline: In the southwest, while Moroni is away, internal Nephite problems allow the Lamanites to take possession of several Nephite cities.

The Ammonites are tempted to take up arms to help defend the Nephites who have been protecting them. Helaman, Alma's son and the High Priest over the Church, and his brethren persuade them not to break their oath.

Two thousand of the sons of the Ammonites, who were too young to take the oath, covenant to take up arms to defend their country. Helaman is made the leader of these valiant and faithful stripling warriors according to their desire. This small army of youth marches to the southwest to the city of Judea, arriving at a critical time to reinforce the Nephite army there. Their arrival causes the Lamanites to quit advancing and concentrate on holding the cities they have already taken. Provisions and other forces, including sixty more Ammonite sons, arrive to strengthen the Nephites.

By stratagem, the strongest Lamanite army is lured out of the city of Antiparah to pursue Helaman and his young warriors. Antipus, with his Nephite army, then follows after the Lamanites. For three days, the three groups march, daring not to turn to the right or the left. When the Lamanites halt their pursuit, Helaman asks his "sons" if they are willing to fight, not knowing whether there is a trap or if Antipus has engaged the enemy from the rear.

With courage and faith in their mothers' words that God would deliver them, these inexperienced fighters turn back and attack the Lamanites. They arrive just in time: the Lamanites are overcoming the forces of Antipus. Helaman's warriors fight with miraculous strength causing the Lamanites to surrender. Also miraculously, not one of the two thousand falls in battle.

The Lamanite prisoners are sent to Zarahemla, and Helaman marches his small army back to the city of Judea. In subsequent battles, the Lord continues to support Helaman's faithful, young warriors. Though they receive many wounds, none of the 2,060 sons are slain.

Gospel Principles:

1. **Compassion.** The people of Ammon were full of feeling for the Nephites who were undergoing tribulation in order to defend them. (See Alma 53:13; 56:7.)

2. **Courage.** Though inexperienced in battle, the 2,060 young warriors showed extraordinary faith and courage. (See Alma 53:20; 56:43-48 and 56; 58:39-40.)

3. **Covenants.** Helaman feared the eternal consequences of the people of Ammon breaking their oath. (See Alma 53:11-15; 56:6-8.)

4. **Faith.** Helaman's young Ammonite soldiers did not doubt that they would be delivered as their mothers had taught them. What examples of faith! (See Alma 56:46-48 and 56; 57:21 and 26-27; 58:39-40.)

5. **Parenthood.** These young men had been taught faith and obedience in their childhood by their parents. (See Alma 53:21; 56:47-48.)

6. **Relief.** In two instances, Helaman's army brought encouragement and reinforcement to Antipus and his disheartened forces. (See Alma 56:15-17 and 49-54.) A visit or a phone call to someone who is struggling can have the same effect, giving the person added strength to go on.

7. **Steadfastness.** Compare the weakness of the Nephites who could not remain true in Moroni's absence with Helaman's stripling sons who were true at all times. (See Alma 53:8-9 and 20-21; 57:21 and 26-27; 58:39-40.)

8. **Temptation.** When pursued by temptation we would do well to follow the example of the fleeing armies in this story. They

dared not turn to the right nor the left but continued in a straight course. (See Alma 56:37 and 40.)

9. **Weakness.** Internal weakness can put you in a dangerous situation. But, by relying upon the Lord, you can receive the strength and protection you need. (See Alma 53:8-9; 56:18-19.)

* * *

STORY 52

HELAMAN'S SMALL FORCE TAKES BACK THE CITY OF MANTI

Reference: Alma 58:1-41

Background: *The Lamanite armies gained possession of several Nephite cities both in the east and the west. Helaman went with his two thousand stripling warriors to strengthen the Nephite forces in the southwest. (See Story 51.) He wrote a letter to Moroni, who was leading the Nephite armies in the east, telling how they took back several of the cities from the Lamanites. (See Alma 56 and 57.)*

Story Outline: Helaman continues his epistle to Moroni. One more city, Manti, remains in the possession of the Lamanites. It is strongly fortified so that the Nephites dare not attack. And, the Lamanites are wise to attempts to lure them out of their strongholds. A stalemate exists.

Helaman sends to Zarahemla for help, provisions, and reinforcements. After waiting for several months, he is disappointed to receive only two thousand soldiers to fulfill his request. Turning to God in earnest prayer, the Nephites are assured that they will be delivered from their enemies, notwithstanding their small force.

When the Lamanite spies discover how small the army is that surrounds the city of Manti, they make preparations to come out to battle against the Nephites. Helaman prepares by splitting two groups off from the main body, one on the right and one on the left. After the huge Lamanite army passes by in pursuit of Helaman, these two side forces fall back and take the lightly guarded city.

When the pursuit ceases because Helaman leads them too close to the Nephite stronghold of Zarahemla, the Lamanites halt and set up camp. But, Helaman and his men march back through the night by another route and return to Manti ahead of their pursuers. The Lamanites, upon finding the Nephites secure in their former strongholds in the city, flee into the wilderness in fear. Thus, the city of Manti is delivered without the shedding of blood, and the Nephites are in possession of all of the cities in that part of the land that had been taken by the Lamanites. Thus, Helaman ends his epistle.

Gospel Principles:

1. **Diligence.** The Nephites had a fixed determination to conquer their enemies. Going the extra mile by marching all night while the Lamanites slept gave them the edge and the victory. (See v. 12 and 25-29.)

2. **Faith.** Helaman said that faith was granted unto them from God. That is an interesting way to look at it. (See v. 10-12.) We can pray for faith to be granted unto us.

3. **Peace.** Even in the difficult circumstances of war, the Nephites received peace in their souls through answers to prayer. (See v. 7 and 10-11.)

4. **Prayer.** The Nephites were earnest in their prayers: they poured out their souls. And, the answer they received was sweet. (See v. 9-12.)

5. **Trust in God.** Finding themselves in dire circumstances, the Nephites realized that they could not depend upon the arm of flesh. They had to turn to the Lord for help. Then their trust and faith became firm and strong. (See v. 2-11, 33 and 37.)

* * *

MORONI LEAVES THE BATTLEFIELD TO RE-ESTABLISH THE GOVERNMENT

Reference: Alma 59:1-13; 60:1-36; 61:1-21; 62:1-11

Background: *The Nephites were attacked and lost cities to the Lamanites on the east and on the west. Helaman, with the help of the Lord and his 2,060 stripling warriors, successfully took back the cities in the west. In an epistle to Chief Captain Moroni who was battling in the east, Helaman told of his success and of his disappointment at the lack of support from Zarahemla, the capital city. (See Story 52.)*

Story Outline: Moroni and his people rejoice over Helaman's success. In an epistle to Chief Judge Pahoran in Zarahemla, Moroni requests men to be sent to Helaman to maintain the regained cities.

While Moroni is making plans to take back the occupied cities in the east, those Lamanites who were driven out by Helaman come join their brothers in this part of the land. The city of Nephihah falls into the hands of the strengthened Lamanite force.

Moroni is angry at the seeming indifference of the government. In a scathing letter to Pahoran he condemns the leaders for neglecting the defense of their country, threatening to come destroy them if they do not send men and provisions immediately.

Pahoran writes to Moroni in reply, saying that he has been deposed from the judgement-seat by rebels who have taken over the city of Zarahemla. He asks for Moroni to come to him that they might drive out these rebels who have appointed a king and made alliance with the King of the Lamanites.

Moroni, glad to hear that Pahoran remains faithful, goes to his aid. Along the way, he raises the standard of liberty (see Story 47) and gathers thousands to fight for freedom.

Pahoran and Moroni join forces. Together they attack and defeat the rebels in Zarahemla. Pahoran is restored to the judgement-seat, and those who remain rebellious are executed.

Gospel Principles:

1. **Communication.** Moroni incorrectly perceived that the government was sitting idle rather than supporting the Nephite armies. In his letter he used some harsh words against Pahoran, even intimating that he was a traitor. Pahoran was big enough to realize why Moroni was upset and did not take offense. Most people would have answered with spite. (See Alma 59:13; 60:6 and 18; 61:9.) Communication, especially between spouses, really breaks down if neither party is willing to see the position of the other.

2. **Forgiveness.** Pahoran gives us an excellent example of forbearance. Though vigorously and falsely accused, he let it go, telling his accuser that "it mattereth not." Righteous rejoicing overshadowed anger. (See Alma 61:9.)

3. **Industry.** Even though Moroni misjudged Pahoran, his advice is good for those who would accomplish something: to "begin to

be up and doing." The Lord expects us to use the means He has provided for us. (See Alma 60:21-24.)

4. **Judging.** It is easy to draw the wrong conclusions, as did Moroni, when we do not know all of the circumstances behind someone else's actions.

5. **Leadership.** Moroni was able to gather thousands around the standard of freedom as he marched toward the land of Gideon. (See Alma 62:3-5.)

6. **Reward for wickedness.** Moroni and his captains felt that the success of their enemies was due to the wickedness of the Nephite people in general. Nevertheless, the distinction was made that those individuals killed in battle were not necessarily the wicked ones. (See Alma 59:11-12; 60:12-13 and 15.)

* * *

STORY 54

THE LONG WAR IS BROUGHT TO AN END

Reference: Alma 62:12-52

Background: *Support, in the form of men and provisions, was not forthcoming from the government in Zarahemla to the soldiers trying to drive out the Lamanites who had taken possession of several Nephite cities. Moroni, Chief Captain of the Nephite armies, was compelled to leave the battle front and return to Zarahemla to help Pahoran, the Chief Judge, who had been deposed by rebels. Together, Moroni and Pahoran, with the forces they gathered, overcame the rebellion. (See Story 53.)*

Story Outline: Moroni sends provisions and men to strengthen Lehi and Teancum who were left in charge of the armies in the east while he was gone. Pahoran and Moroni march a large army to the land of Nephihah, defeating a large army of Lamanites along the way.

By night, the Nephites sneak in over the wall that surrounds the city of Nephihah, on the side opposite from where the Lamanites are camped. In the morning, the Lamanites are surprised to find their enemies inside their city and flee before the Nephites. Many Lamanites are slain and taken prisoner. Those who are desirous to give up their weapons and join the people of Ammon in the land of Jershon (see Story 43) are freed.

With his army strengthened by former Nephite prisoners, Moroni pursues the Lamanites, driving them from city to city, even unto the land of Moroni on the southeast border. There the forces of Lehi and Teancum join with Moroni in surrounding the combined Lamanite army.

Teancum sneaks into the Lamanite camp by night and kills Ammoron, the Lamanite king, in his sleep. But, Teancum is slain in return before he can escape. On the morrow, Moroni attacks and drives the Lamanites completely out of the Nephite lands.

Thus, after many years of internal strife and war with the Lamanites, peace is once again established amongst the Nephites. Captain Moroni, the valiant warrior, retires. Pahoran returns to his judgement-seat. And, Helaman goes back to preaching the word of God. There is a regulation in the Church and the law. The people remain humble and prayerful as the Lord blesses them with prosperity.

Gospel Principles:

1. **Attitude.** Isn't it interesting that the same set of circumstances can harden some people and soften others? How we react depends upon our outlook. (See v. 41.)

2. **Forgiveness.** What a wonderful way to get rid of enemies – forgive them and let them go free as friends! (See v. 15-17 and 27-29.)

3. **Humility.** Here we see two different conditions, under which some of the Nephites were able to remain humble. In afflictions they became softened, not hardened; in prosperity, they avoided pride. (See v. 41 and 48-51.)

4. **Prayer.** The prayers of the righteous prevented the utter destruction of the Nephites in their wickedness. And, in their prosperity, the Nephites remembered to pray continually. (See v. 40 and 51.)

5. **Remembrance.** The Nephites at this period were unusual. During their prosperity, they did not forget the Lord and what He had done for them. (See v. 48-51.)

6. **Reward for righteousness.** The Nephites were spared because of the prayers of the righteous amongst them. (See v. 40.)

7. **Temptation.** Temptation comes in the dark. If we let down our guard, sin will sneak inside. All of the Lamanites were asleep. Was it apathy or overconfidence? They knew the enemy was camped round about them, but they neglected to take the proper precautions. When temptation surrounds us we have to be extra cautious. (See v. 20-24.)

* * *

STORY 55

PROSPERITY AMONGST THE NEPHITES LEADS TO PRIDE AND DEFEAT

Reference: Helaman 3:22-37; 4:1-26

Background: *Over a period of several years, various contentions and wars arose amongst the Nephites in the land of Zarahemla. (See Alma 63:14-16 and Helaman 1:1-34; 2:1-14; 3:1-3 and 17-20.)*

Story Outline: The contentions wane, and peace and prosperity settle in. Thousands repent and join the Church. Blessings are poured out upon the Church and all of the Nephites.

After a few years of peace and joy, pride starts to creep in because of riches and prosperity. As pride grows, peace is choked out until contentions result in bloodshed. Dissenters go up from the Nephites and persuade the Lamanites to come to battle against the Nephites. The Nephites lose the land of Zarahemla to their enemies and are forced northward.

Because of the preaching of Moronihah and of Nephi and Lehi many Nephites repent, but not all. The Nephites' strength over their enemies is in proportion to their righteousness. Moronihah, now commanding the Nephite armies in place of his father, Moroni, succeeds in regaining half of the property that the Lamanites had taken. But, because of unrighteousness, the Nephite people have not enough strength to regain all of their lands.

Gospel Principles:

1. **Adversity.** By turning their hearts unto God through fasting and prayer, the faithful saints gained strength and consolation during their persecutions and afflictions. (See Helaman 3:34-35.)

2. **Confidence.** When the Nephites were wicked, their confidence did not wax strong in the presence of the Lord. (See Helaman 4:13 and 23-26.)

3. **Crime.** Then, just as now, robbery thrived more in the cities than in the less populated areas. (See Helaman 3:23.)

4. **Fasting.** Fasting and prayer helped the faithful saints to endure persecutions and affliction. (See Helaman 3:34-35.)

5. **Forgetfulness.** In the space of ten years, the Nephites changed their state from joy and peace to weakness and fear. Pride caused them to forget God, His laws, and His commandments. (See Helaman 3:32; 4:20-26.)

6. **Hypocrisy.** The church members were the ones who became proud and oppressed the poor. They should have been setting the example for righteousness not wickedness. (See Helaman 4:11-12.)

7. **Pride.** Pride creeps in slowly at first. But, if left unchecked, it grows like cancer until the entire nation is threatened. (See Helaman 3:33-34 and 36; 4:1-2 and 12.)

* * *

STORY 56

NEPHI AND LEHI DEDICATE THEMSELVES TO PREACHING THE WORD

Reference: Helaman 5:1-52

Background: *Prosperity amongst the Nephites led to pride, which caused them to fall into a state of wickedness and unbelief. (See Story 55.) Nephi, Helaman's eldest son, reigned as chief judge in place of his father who died. (See Helaman 4:37.)*

Story Outline: Nephi gives up the judgement-seat. He and his brother, Lehi, devote the rest of their lives to preaching the word of God. In so doing, they remember and honor the admonition and instruction given them by their father, Helaman. They preach with power as they visit city after city amongst the Nephites and Lamanites in the land of Zarahemla. Amongst the many who repent and are baptized are eight thousand Lamanites.

As Nephi and Lehi go into the land of Nephi to continue their preaching, they are captured and imprisoned by a Lamanite army. When their captors come to the prison to slay them, they find the two men encircled about with a protective pillar of fire. Nephi and Lehi stand forth and declare that this marvel is from God. The earth quakes and a cloud of darkness covers the prison. Three times, a voice from above calls the Lamanites to repentance. Though the voice is mild, its power shakes the earth and the prison walls.

Aminadab, a Nephite dissenter and former church member, observes through the dark cloud the brightly shining faces of the two missionaries as they converse with angels. He shows the multitude what he sees and tells them to pray and repent, having faith in Christ, to make the cloud of darkness disperse.

Those in the prison cry unto the Lord and the darkness does disperse. All the people are encircled with fire and filled with joy and the Holy Ghost. They hear a voice proclaiming peace. The heavens are opened and angels come down and minister to them.

The three hundred souls who witness these marvelous things tell others throughout the region. Most of the Lamanites are converted and lay down their arms.

Gospel Principles:

1. **Activation.** Aminadab is an example of a sheep that had strayed being called back into service to bring others into the fold. (See v. 35-41.)

2. **Commitment.** Nephi and Lehi dedicated the rest of their lives to preaching the word of God. (See v. 4.)

3. **Jesus Christ.** As the three hundred Lamanites did, we can bring light and peace into our lives by having faith to build upon Christ as our foundation. (See v. 12, 41-43 and 47.)

4. **Missionary work.** As a result of their powerful preaching, Nephi and Lehi had great success in converting Nephites and Lamanites. Their power and their words were given to them from God. (See v. 17-19.)

5. **Parenthood.** Helaman was wise to give his sons exemplary names that would remind them of how they should act. (See v. 6-7.)

6. **Power of God.** We see many examples of God's power in this story: inspired words that confound and convert, miraculous signs of fire, earthquake and cloud, and a piercing, yet mild, voice. (See v. 17-19, 23, 27-34 and 43-48.)

7. **Remembrance.** These two faithful sons remembered and honored the words of their father, Helaman. (See v. 13-14.)

8. **Repentance.** Those who were converted, both Nephites and Lamanites, sought to right their previous wrongs as part of their repentance. The Lamanite converts restored to the Nephites the lands of their possession. (See v. 17 and 51-52.)

9. **Teaching.** In this story, there opened up two prime teaching windows: a) for Nephi and Lehi when encircled about with a pillar of fire, and b) for Aminadab when the faces of Nephi and Lehi shone through the cloud of darkness. The wise teachers, as guided by the Spirit, seized their moments and were successful. (See v. 24-26 and 35-41.)

* * *

NEPHITE PEACE IS DESTROYED BY THE GADIANTON ROBBERS

Reference: Helaman 6:1-40

Background: *Due to the preaching of Nephi and Lehi, the more part of the Lamanites repented and were converted. (See Story 56.)*

Story Outline: The faithfulness and righteousness of the Lamanites exceed those of the Nephites. Many of the Lamanites come and preach amongst the Nephites. Peace abounds throughout the land. There is free commerce between the two peoples. It is a time of joy and prosperity.

After a few years, the peace is disturbed by Gadianton's band of robbers. Two assassinations are carried out, on Cezoram, the Chief Judge, and then on his son after he succeeds to the judgement-seat. Because of secret combinations, the murderers are not found.

The Nephite people set their hearts on riches and become wicked. The Gadiantons flourish amongst them as more and more join and take the secret oaths. This evil band obtains control of the government. An awful state exists in which the humble and meek are oppressed.

As the Nephites become more wicked and the Spirit of the Lord withdraws from them, the Lamanites increase in righteousness and spirituality. The Lamanites utterly destroy the Gadianton band from amongst them by preaching the word of God to the more wicked. The Spirit is poured out upon the Lamanites.

Gospel Principles:

1. **Holy Ghost.** A standard for receiving the Spirit is outlined. We must be open, willing, and teachable. (See v. 35-36.)

2. **Preaching.** What a unique way to get rid of criminals: preach the gospel to them. (See v. 37.)

3. **Repentance.** The first steps to making things right are to recognize what is wrong and to feel sorry for it. The Lamanites took those steps and rooted out the evil; the Nephites did not. (See v. 20-21 and 37-38.)

4. **Riches.** The people's blessings came from God. But, their unappreciative hearts turned to the gifts themselves rather than to the Giver of the gifts. (See v. 16-17.)

5. **Satan.** Those involved in sin have something to hide. Satan's work is done in secret and darkness. (See v. 26-30.)

6. **Sin.** It does not take long for sin to spread if it is left unchecked. (See v. 32.)

* * *

STORY 58

NEPHI REVEALS THE MURDER OF THE CHIEF JUDGE

Reference: Helaman 7:1-20; 8:1-11 and 27-28; 9:1-41; 10:1-19

Background: *The Nephites were in a more wicked condition than the Lamanites. The secret Gadianton society thrived, taking over the Nephite government. (See Story 57.)*

Story Outline: Nephi returns to Zarahemla from the land northward where his preaching was wholly rejected. Heavy with sorrow for the iniquities of his people, he wishes for a better day. He pours out his soul to God from the tower in his garden, which is near a main highway. Passersby gather around to see the cause of such great lamentation.

When Nephi beholds the gathered multitude, he addresses them, pointing out their sins, and calling upon them to repent lest they should lose their lands and be destroyed. (See Helaman 7:13-29.) Judges, who are members of the Gadianton band, stir up the people to anger against Nephi. But, many in the crowd support him and his words, so he continues preaching. (See Helaman 8:11-26.)

Nephi points out the many prophets who have testified of the coming of Christ. Then, as a sign, he announces the murder of the Chief Judge in the judgement-seat.

Five men run to the judgement-seat to see if Nephi is right. When they see the Chief Judge lying dead in his blood, they fall to the earth realizing that Nephi's words about the Nephites' destruction are true. These unconscious runners are discovered by the people who answer the cry of the servants of the Chief Judge. The five are accused of the murder and are imprisoned.

The next day at the burial of the Chief Judge, those judges who had heard Nephi in his garden inquire about the five men who were sent. The judges find out that the five have been arrested and ask to have them brought for questioning. After telling their story, the five men are acquitted and released.

The judges then claim that Nephi is responsible for the murder. Over the protests of the five witnesses, Nephi is bound and brought before the judges where he is accused.

Nephi again tells them to repent or be destroyed. He gives them a second sign. They are to go to the brother of the slain man and ask him specific questions about the murder. Nephi prophesies the brother's answers, in first denying the deed and then confessing it, when confronted with the blood stain on his cloak. They go to the brother and find that he acts just as Nephi said he would.

Nephi is freed. Some of the people believe he is a prophet; others say he is a god. The people disperse.

Nephi, left alone, goes toward his home. On the way, as he is pondering, the voice of God comes unto him. He is given great power over the earth and the people. Without going home first, he returns to the multitude and delivers the message that the voice commanded: repent or be destroyed.

The Nephites harden their hearts and will not hearken to Nephi's words. When they seek to lay hands on him to cast him into prison, he is safely carried out of their midst by the Spirit.

Gospel Principles:

1. **Diligence.** Nephi was greatly rewarded for his perseverance in declaring the word. (See Helaman 10:4-5.)

2. **Divine guidance.** Nephi was guided by the Spirit to the extent of delivery from physical harm. (See Helaman 10:16-17.)

3. **Forgetfulness.** All of us, like Nephi, have longed for the good old days. But, we forget that there were plenty of problems in previous times. Nephi was not remembering all of the rebelliousness of Laman and Lemuel and their people. (See Helaman 7:7-9.)

4. **Guilt.** One who is guilty of a crime stands on shaky ground. (See Helaman 9:29-35.) Only through repentance and virtue can we stand confidently before God. (See *D&C* 121:45-46.)

5. **Hardheartedness.** When Nephi spoke plainly to the multitude about their sins, there were two different reactions. The Gadianton judges were angry and wanted Nephi stopped. Others, with more open hearts and minds, accepted what he said as truth and were willing to listen. (See Helaman 8:1-10; 9:39.)

6. **Obedience.** Nephi did not hesitate. When he was commanded by the Lord he obeyed right away without returning to his personal affairs first. (See Helaman 10:11-12.)

7. **Pondering.** Revelation often comes, as in this case with Nephi, during pondering. (See Helaman 10:2-3.) Take time to think about the word of God and listen to His voice.

8. **Power of God.** Nephi was miraculously protected, conveyed by the Spirit out of their midst so that he could not be imprisoned. (See Helaman 10:16.)

9. **Revelation.** The murder of the Chief Judge was only a part of what was revealed to Nephi, only a sign to the people that his words were true. The greater part was found in his preaching and exhortations. (See Helaman 8:27-28; 9:2 and 36.)

10. **Sign seeking.** The people desired proof of Nephi's words, but they were not converted by the miracle he showed them. (See Helaman 9:2 and 23-24; 10:13.)

11. **Teaching.** Nephi took advantage of the teaching opportunities that came his way on his garden tower and before the judges. (See Helaman 7:11-13; 8:10-11.)

12. **Trust in God.** Those who start thinking that they are more powerful and great than God are setting themselves up for a fall. (See Helaman 8:5-6.)

13. **Unity.** Nephi was so much in harmony with the Lord that he was granted power that all things would be done according to his word. (See Helaman 10:5.)

* * *

STORY 59

NEPHI ASKS FOR A FAMINE
TO HUMBLE THE NEPHITES

Reference: Helaman 11:1-21

Background: *Because Nephi was so diligent in crying repentance unto the wicked Nephites, God's voice came to him, blessed him, and gave him great power over the earth and the people. Nephi spread the word of God amongst all of the Nephites, but they would not hearken unto him. (See Story 58.)*

Story Outline: Contentions and bloodshed increase amongst the Nephites. The Gadianton band of robbers is the cause of a war that lasts more than a year.

Nephi calls upon God to send a famine in the land. It is done according to his words. The source of the destruction of the people changes from sword to famine. Many perish.

Finally, the Nephites repent and turn back to God. The Gadiantons are eliminated. The people ask their leaders to get Nephi to pray for the famine to end. The rains come according to Nephi's prayer, and the earth brings forth abundance again.

The people rejoice and glorify God. They esteem Nephi as a great prophet. With the greater part of the Nephites and Lamanites belonging to the Church, peace and prosperity abound.

Gospel Principles:

1. **Contention.** The Devil is the father of contention. By using the secret band of robbers, he sharpened the contentions to the point of civil war. (See v. 1-2.)

2. **Faith.** Nephi knew that the Lord would honor his words to begin and end the famine. (See v. 14. Also see Helaman 10:6-10.)

3. **Power of God.** At length, the people realized that the famine was controlled by the power of God given to Nephi. (See v. 18.)

4. **Prophets.** The dealings between the Lord and the Nephites were done through the prophet Nephi. (See v. 4-5, 8-9 and 18. Also see Helaman 10:6-11.)

5. **Repentance.** It took a sore famine to make the Nephites remember their God. How much tribulation does it take to humble us and bring us to repentance? (See v. 4, 7 and 9.)

* * *

STORY 60

THE NEPHITES TURN AWAY FROM GOD AGAIN

Reference: Helaman 11:22-38; 12:1-6

Background: *The wicked Gadianton band was the cause of serious internal wars amongst the Nephites. The prophet, Nephi, called for a sore famine in the land, which eventually humbled the people and brought them to repentance. The famine was then replaced by peace and prosperity. (See Story 59.)*

Story Outline: Peace continues except for some doctrinal contentions. Through revelation and preaching, Nephi and Lehi put an end to the strife.

A band of Nephite dissenters and Lamanites resurrect the secret plans of Gadianton and begin to war against the Nephites and the Lamanites. Attempts by armies to destroy this band, hiding out in the wilderness and mountains, are unsuccessful. The robbers increase in strength and numbers.

At first, the people remember their God when they are persecuted by the robbers. But gradually, pride and wickedness creep in until the people are ripening for destruction again.

Mormon, the abridger of the record, reflects on the unsteadiness and forgetfulness of man.

<u>Gospel Principles:</u>

1. **Choosing the right.** The dissenters grew in numbers as more and more people chose evil over good. (See Helaman 11:25-26 and 32.) Which side are you on?

2. **Contention.** Satan, the father of contention, would have us dispute what the prophets tell us. (See Helaman 11:22.)

3. **Forgetfulness.** How easy it is to forget the Lord when things are going well. Where are we now in the cycle of chastisement, repentance, blessing, prosperity, forgetting, wickedness, and chastisement? (See Helaman 11:34-37; 12:1-6.)

4. **Preaching.** Preaching has the power to end strife. (See Helaman 11:23.)

5. **Prosperity.** Prosperity is a two-edged sword; it comes at once as blessing and trial. The test of prosperity is difficult: remaining humble and remembering the Lord when we may think our blessings are coming from our own labor. (See Helaman 12:1-6.)

6. **Revelation.** Nephi, Lehi, and their brethren had to be in tune with the Spirit to receive many revelations daily. (See Helaman 11:23.)

7. **Satan.** Satan operates in secrecy and darkness. (See Helaman 11:26.)

8. **Steadfastness.** When these people put their hands to the plow they did not hold on. In a few short years, they forgot and turned from their commitments to the Lord. (See Helaman 11:34-37; 12:1-6.)

* * *

STORY 61

SAMUEL THE LAMANITE PROPHESIES TO THE NEPHITES

Reference: Helaman 13:1-14; 14:1-15 and 20-31; 16:1-8

Background: *Despite the preaching of Nephi and Lehi, wickedness and pride increased amongst the Nephites. The secret Gadianton band of robbers thrived again. (See Story 60.)*

Story Outline: The Lamanites remain obedient to God's commandments while the Nephites increase in wickedness. Samuel, a Lamanite, comes amongst the Nephites preaching repentance, but he is cast out. The voice of the Lord tells him to return and prophesy whatever comes into his heart.

Since the Nephites will not let Samuel enter Zarahemla, he climbs up on the wall of the city and boldly declares unto them the things the Lord puts into his heart. He prophesies of heavy destruction within four hundred years if the people do not repent and turn to Christ. The city is spared now only for the sake of those righteous who are in it.

Samuel condemns the Nephites for setting their hearts on riches and for casting out the prophets, seeking flattering words instead. They are to be cursed with slippery possessions. (See Helaman 13:15-39.)

Samuel prophesies of the coming of Christ. His birth in five years will be heralded by signs in the heavens: a new star and no darkness on the night before He comes into the world. The signs of Christ's death are also foretold, including: three days of darkness, tempests, earthquakes, and resurrection of dead saints. Samuel emphasizes free agency: we can choose either good or evil, life or death. He prophesies more about the Nephite destruction and of the preservation of a Lamanite remnant in the latter days. (See Helaman 15.)

Some Nephites believe Samuel's words, repent, and seek baptism at the hand of Nephi. But, the non-believers are angry. They cast stones and shoot arrows at Samuel. The Spirit protects him so that he cannot be hit. This miracle produces more believers who go to Nephi to be baptized.

The majority of the people, however, do not believe. They cry to their captains to capture the man since they cannot hit him with stones and arrows. But, Samuel jumps down from the wall and returns to his own land, never to be heard of again amongst the Nephites.

(See Stories 62, 65, and 70 for the fulfillment of Samuel's prophecies.)

Gospel Principles:

1. **Accountability.** With freedom of choice comes responsibility for the results. The signs of Christ's coming were given that all would have the chance to believe. (See Helaman 14:28-31.)

2. **Conversion.** The invitation was made to all, but only some believed. Samuel's miraculous protection helped others to believe. (See Helaman 16:1-5.)

3. **Diligence.** Barred from the city, Samuel did not give up. He climbed up on the wall to deliver his divine message. (See Helaman 13:4.)

4. **Free agency.** We, like the Nephites, are free to choose for ourselves. We also know good from evil. (See Helaman 14:29-31.)

5. **Jesus Christ.** What wondrous signs were given to announce these most important events in all history! (See Helaman 14:3-8 and 20-28.)

6. **Justice.** We will be fairly judged on our choices between good and evil. (See Helaman 14:29-31.)

7. **Mercy.** The tempests and earthquakes, though devastating, were to come with the intent of helping the people believe in Christ. (See Helaman 14:28-29.)

8. **Prophecy.** How remarkable and unique that Samuel foretold the exact time that the Savior would come into the world! Can you imagine what it would be like if our prophet told us that Christ would come again to the earth after "five years more?" (See Helaman 14:2.)

9. **Revelation.** The Lord put into the heart of His prophet what was to be said to His people. Such is the pattern of revelation to the world: from God to the prophet to the people. (See Helaman 13:3 and 5; 14:9.)

10. **Reward for righteousness.** The Lord has respect for the righteous. He spared the great city of Zarahemla only because of the righteous who dwelt therein. (See Helaman 13:12-14.)

11. **Straight-and-narrow way.** Many heard Samuel's words, some believed, but many more did not. (See Helaman 16:1-2 and 6.)

12. **Warning.** In His infinite mercy, the Lord sent Samuel to the Nephites to give a voice of warning that if they would not repent they would be utterly destroyed. (See Helaman 13:8-11; 15:17.)

* * *

STORY 62

THE SIGNS OF CHRIST'S BIRTH COME TO PASS

Reference: Helaman 16:10-24; 3 Nephi 1:4-23

Background: *Samuel the Lamanite preached to the Nephites from the wall surrounding the city of Zarahemla. He prophesied that the Savior would come into the world in five years and that great signs would attend His coming. (See Story 61.) Nephi, son of Helaman, gave charge of the plates to his son Nephi. (See 3 Nephi 1:2.)*

Story Outline: The majority of the Nephites remain proud and wicked, becoming even more hardened in iniquity. Two years before the birth of Christ, great signs and wonders are given, including angels appearing unto men. Except for the most believing amongst the Nephites and Lamanites, the people harden their hearts and try to rationalize away the signs. Rumors spread, contentions arise, and Satan rages.

In the year before Christ's birth, greater signs and miracles are wrought amongst the people. Some say that the time predicted by Samuel is past. The unbelievers persecute the believers who hold to the hope of the prophesied day and a night and a day with no darkness. A day is set by the unbelievers that, if the sign does not come to pass, the believers shall be put to death.

Nephi, son of Nephi, is sorrowed because of this wickedness. All day, in mighty prayer, he bows himself before the Lord on behalf of those who are about to be destroyed because of their faith. The voice of the Lord comes to Nephi, cheering him, saying that the sign will be given this night and on the morrow He will come into the world.

At sunset, there is no darkness. The people fall to the earth in astonishment. They realize that the Son of God must shortly appear. They are struck with fear because of their iniquity and unbelief. A new star also appears. When the sun rises, they know that it is the day of the Savior's birth.

The majority of the people are converted to the Lord despite the efforts of Satan in spreading lies to deceive and cause disbelief in the signs. Many people are baptized by Nephi and others. Peace returns to the land.

Gospel Principles:

1. **Deception.** The great deceiver, Satan, can cause all kinds of rationalizations, that the people will be drawn away from what is truly happening. (See Helaman 16:15-23.)

2. **Faith.** The strength of faith and hope had to rise in proportion to the increase of persecution. Our faith will be tried. (See 3 Nephi 1:7-9.)

3. **Fear.** The fear that the wicked felt must be similar to what we will feel if we are not prepared to meet God. When the day of judgement arrives, the time for preparation is past. (See 3 Nephi 1:16-18.)

4. **Jesus Christ.** What a marvelous thing, that the premortal Lord's voice should announce His entry into the world on the night before it happened! (See 3 Nephi 1:12-14.)

5. **Persecution.** Wicked men take pride in persecuting the saints. Look how the persecution escalated, even unto a death penalty. Yet, what harm was caused the non-believers by the humble faith of the followers of Christ? It is plain to see that the architect of persecution is Satan, the father of contention. (See 3 Nephi 1:5-9.)

6. **Prayer.** It was no quick or weak prayer that Nephi offered. All the day long he cried mightily unto the Lord on behalf of his people. (See 3 Nephi 1:10-13.)

7. **Prophecy.** The words of the prophets are fulfilled even if men doubt or ignore or think the time is past. (See Helaman 16:13-16; 3 Nephi 1:4-5.)

8. **Repentance.** Repentance by the people brought peace into the land. (See 3 Nephi 1:23.)

9. **Satan.** Lies, rumors, deceit, contention, these are the tools used by Satan to draw people away from the true light. (See Helaman 16:22; 3 Nephi 1:22.)

10. **Trust in God.** Too often, people rationalize away the things that God does rather than realizing that He is the one in control of all things. (See Helaman 16:15-22.)

11. **Wonders.** The magnitude of the signs and wonders given was suited to this event, one of the greatest moments in total world history, the birth of the Son of God upon the earth. (See 3 Nephi 1:15-21.)

* * *

STORY 63

THE NEPHITES AND LAMANITES BATTLE THE GADIANTON ROBBERS

Reference: 3 Nephi 1:27-30; 2:1-3 and 10-13; 3:1-26; 4:1-33; 5:1-6

Background: *The foretold signs of Christ's birth were given just in time to save the believers from martyrdom. Many people were converted, and peace was restored to the land. (See Story 62.)*

Story Outline: The peace is disturbed by the Gadianton robbers who murder and then return to their secret strongholds in the mountains. The numbers of this secret band increase as both Nephites and Lamanites dissent and join them. The people forget and begin to disbelieve the signs of Christ's birth that they had seen. Wickedness abounds.

The Gadiantons become so strong and numerous that the Lamanites must unite and take up arms with the Nephites for self-preservation. The war escalates between the augmented numbers of the Nephites and the Gadiantons.

Giddianhi, leader of the robbers, writes an epistle to Lachoneus, Governor of the land, threatening the extinction of the Nephites unless they surrender. Lachoneus, a just man, does not yield to the robbers. Instead, he prepares his people, calling on them to repent and ask for God's help. Fearing the Governor's words and prophecies, the people obey him by repenting and making ready for war. Lachoneus gathers all those who are called Nephites to one central location. Gidgiddoni, a great prophet amongst them, is appointed to be chief captain.

The robbers try to possess the lands vacated by the Nephites, but there are no crops nor flocks left behind, nothing for them to plunder. A year later, in order to survive, the Gadiantons are forced to attack the large, gathered body of Nephites. The appearance of the robbers in armor is fierce and frightening. The Nephites fall to the ground in supplication to the Lord. The attackers, thinking their victims are afraid, are surprised when they are met with the strength of the Lord. The battle is severe. The Nephites drive the robbers back and pursue them, slaying their leader, Giddianhi, along with many others.

Two years later, under a new leader, Zemnarihah, the robbers lay siege around the centralized Nephites. But, the Nephites are well provisioned. It is the robbers, depending on the vanishing wild game, who suffer from hunger and are the objects of raids wherein thousands are slain. Therefore, Zemnarihah orders a retreat. But, Gidgiddoni anticipates their movement and moves his armies by night to cut off their path from both sides. In the morning, the robbers are surrounded. Those who do not surrender are slain, and their leader is hung.

The Nephites rejoice and give praise and thanks to God for delivering them from their enemies. All of the Nephites believe in the prophecies of Christ, and they serve God. The robber prisoners are preached to and freed or punished, according to their willingness to repent.

Gospel Principles:

1. **Deception.** It is interesting how Satan twists things, calling black white and white black. Here he deceives men by saying that the

doctrine of Christ is wrought by the power of the Devil in order to deceive men. (See 3 Nephi 2:1-3.)

2. **Forgetfulness.** Unless we continually renew and strengthen our testimonies, we can become calloused to spiritual things. Our eyes become blind, our hearts become hardened, and we forget those things we formerly knew by the Spirit. (See 3 Nephi 2:1-2.)

3. **Generation gap.** The new generation did not follow in the way of its forbearers. (See 3 Nephi 1:29-30.)

4. **Gratitude.** The Nephites' gratitude was a natural expression of their joy because they knew it was by the power of God that they were delivered. (See 3 Nephi 4:31-33.)

5. **Leadership.** It was a wise policy to choose men of God to lead the people. (See 3 Nephi 3:19.)

6. **Perception.** Trouble between parties often stems from differences in perception. Lachoneus was astonished that the robbers felt that they had been wronged. Have you met inactive church members who shun the Church because they feel that they have been offended? (See 3 Nephi 3:10-11.)

7. **Prayer.** Prayer was a greater protection than armor and fierce appearance. (See 3 Nephi 3:12; 4:7-10.)

8. **Preparation.**
   - Lachoneus caused his people to prepare physically by gathering provisions and spiritually by repenting. (See 3 Nephi 3:12-15; 4:8-10.)
   - Contrast the situation of the robbers with that of the Nephites: the one group not able to sustain life, the other well provisioned for years. (See 3 Nephi 4:4 and 18-20.)

9. **Repentance.** Why does it so often take a crisis to get us to repent and turn to the Lord? (See 3 Nephi 3:15-16 and 25.)

10. **Testimony.** Unless we continually renew and strengthen our testimonies, we can become calloused to spiritual things. Our eyes become blind, our hearts become hardened, and we forget those things we formerly knew by the Spirit. (See 3 Nephi 2:1-2.)

11. **Wonders.** The rapture of seeing a sign or wonder fades over time. So does testimony unless it is constantly reinforced by seeking the Spirit daily. (See 3 Nephi 2:1-2.)

* * *

STORY 64

THE NEPHITE GOVERNMENT IS BROKEN UP

Reference: 3 Nephi 6:1-30; 7:1-26

Background: *After the foretold signs of Christ's birth had come to pass, the peace in the land was disturbed by the murderous Gadianton robbers. The Nephites gathered their provisions and moved to a central place where they were able to outlast and defeat the robbers. (See Story 63.)*

Story Outline: The Nephites return to their own lands. Peace and prosperity abound for a short time. Then, divisions develop between the rich and the poor. Some people are lifted up in pride, while others are exceedingly humble. The Church is broken up because of the inequality and contentions.

Prophets come amongst the Nephites testifying of Christ and His resurrection and redemption. Many of these prophets are put to death illegally by judges who do not get the required permission from the Governor of the land. When these wicked judges are brought to trial, their associates, lawyers, high priests, and judges, combine in a covenant to deliver them and fight against righteousness.

The Chief Judge of the land is murdered. The people are divided. Tribes are formed. The government and its laws are destroyed. All this is because of the secret combination of the friends and kindred of those who murdered the prophets. Contention and wickedness run rampant.

The secret combination chooses a king and moves northward because the other tribes are in greater number. Each tribe has its own laws, yet agrees not to trespass against other tribes. Prophets are stoned and cast out.

By the power of God, Nephi preaches repentance and works great miracles amongst the tribes. Few repent at first, but in the next year, many are baptized.

Gospel Principles:

1. **Charity.** Within four years, this people, who had forgiven the repentant robbers, forgot charity and oppressed the poor. (See 3 Nephi 6:3 and 10-15.)

2. **Forgetfulness.** Within six years, the majority of the Nephites forgot their former deliverance by the Lord. (See 3 Nephi 7:8. Also, see Story 63.)

3. **Law.** The principles and laws of righteous government must be upheld by the citizens or chaos and anarchy will result. (See 3 Nephi 6:4, 22-24 and 30; 7:1-3, 6 and 14.)

4. **Mercy.** Out of love for His children, God sends messengers to those ensnared in wickedness to give them a chance to repent and return to Him. (See 3 Nephi 6:17 and 20; 7:15-16.)

5. **Power of God.** What a powerful ministry Nephi had! He even raised his brother from the dead. (See 3 Nephi 7:15 and 17-20.)

6. **Preparation.** The Nephites prepared so well that they had provisions left over after outlasting the siege. (See 3 Nephi 6:2.)

7. **Pride.** How un-Christlike to consider yourself better than others because your opportunities for education are greater or because you have more wealth. (See 3 Nephi 6:10-15.)

8. **Reward for wickedness.** Peace was lost because of the transgressions of the people. (See 3 Nephi 6:5, 14 and 17.)

9. **Riches.** Beware of riches, the trigger of pride, disputations, persecutions, inequality, and possibly the breakup of government. (See 3 Nephi 6:10-15.)

10. **Sin.** If we have been taught what is right and then choose evil, we are knowingly and willfully rebelling against God – a sobering thought. (See 3 Nephi 6:16-18.)

* * *

THE RESURRECTED CHRIST APPEARS TO THE PEOPLE OF NEPHI

Reference: 3 Nephi 8:2-25; 9:1-22; 10:1-10; 11:1-12

Background: *After the signs of Christ's birth foretold by Samuel, the Lamanite, had come to pass, secret combinations, pride, wickedness, and contentions broke up the Church and the government of the Nephites. (See Stories 61 through 64.)*

Story Outline: The people start looking in earnest for the sign that Samuel the Lamanite predicted: three days of darkness to proclaim Christ's death. During their disagreements and disputations, a great storm arises with thunder, lightning, and earthquakes. Many cities are destroyed, being sunk, buried, or burned. The tempest lasts about three hours. Then, a vapor of darkness, so thick that it can be felt, comes upon the land. For three days there is no light; no fire can be kindled. There is great mourning, howling, and weeping. The survivors cry, "O, that we had repented before this great and terrible day."

The voice of Christ is heard by all the inhabitants of the land, proclaiming the extent of the destruction. Only those people who are more righteous are left. They are called to repent and come unto Christ to be healed. Then there is silence in the land for several hours.

A voice comes again, telling how oft the Lord had tried to gather His people. The people begin again to weep and mourn for the loss of their kindred and friends.

After three days, when the darkness disperses and the earth stops trembling, the mourning and lamentation of the survivors is turned to joy, praise, and thanksgiving.

A large multitude of the people of Nephi is gathered at the temple in the land of Bountiful, talking about what has happened, when a voice from heaven is heard. The people cannot understand the voice, even when it is heard a second time.

The third time, the survivors hear and understand Heavenly Father's voice introducing His Beloved Son. The resurrected Jesus Christ descends out of heaven, clothed in a white robe. He stands in their midst and tells them who He is and that He has finished the work that the Father sent Him to do. The multitude falls to the earth in reverence.

Gospel Principles:

1. **Blindness, Spiritual.** How many times does God have to call us before we will not only hear but understand, three times, more, or fewer? (See 3 Nephi 11:3-7.)

2. **Jesus Christ.** What a glorious and concise description of the Savior and what he has done for mankind is given here! (See 3 Nephi 9:15-22.)

3. **Mercy.** The Lord's arm of mercy is ever extended to those who will come unto Him. (See 3 Nephi 9:14; 10:4-6.)

4. **Prophecy.** The scriptures concerning Christ's first coming were fulfilled. Even so, the prophecies of His Second Coming will come to pass. (See 3 Nephi 9:16; 11:10-11.)

5. **Prophets.** One gets the distinct idea that the Lord wants us to reverence His prophets. (See 3 Nephi 9:10-11.)

6. **Repentance.** The destruction that came upon those who were more wicked reminds us that we should not procrastinate the day of our repentance. Even those who were spared because they were more righteous still needed to repent. (See 3 Nephi 8:24-25; 9:13 and 22.)

7. **Reward for righteousness.** The more righteous people were spared from destruction. (See 3 Nephi 9:12-13.)

8. **Reward for wickedness.** The destruction came upon those who were wicked. (See 3 Nephi 9:2 and 12.)

9. **Temples.** The temple was a place of refuge where the people gathered. When the Savior descended, He came to His house on earth. (See 3 Nephi 11:1 and 8.)

10. **Wonders.** Notice the symbolism in the signs that were given: a night without darkness when the Light of the world was born on the earth, and thick darkness for three days when the Light passed out of the world. (See 3 Nephi 1:19; 8:3 and 20-23.)

* * *

STORY 66

JESUS ESTABLISHES HIS CHURCH

Reference: 3 Nephi 11:13-41; 12:1-2; 18:1-38; 19:4-13; 26:13 and 17-21; 27:1-22; 28:18-23; Moroni 6:1-9

Background: *The foretold signs of Christ's death came to pass: tempests, earthquakes, great destruction, and three days of thick darkness. After being introduced by His Father, the resurrected Lord came down from heaven and stood in the midst of the survivors at the temple in the land of Bountiful. (See Story 65.)*

Story Outline: Upon Jesus' invitation, the entire multitude comes forth. One by one, each person feels the wounds in the Lord's side, hands, and feet.

Jesus calls Nephi and eleven others forth and gives them power to baptize. He makes His doctrine plain to them so that there will not be disputations: belief in Christ, repentance, baptism, and reception of the Holy Ghost are required to inherit the kingdom of God. This is His doctrine, His gospel. He charges the twelve disciples to declare His words unto the ends of the earth.

Jesus repeats the Sermon on the Mount and gives other teachings and instructions to the multitude and the chosen disciples. He administers the emblems of the sacrament to the multitude and tells the twelve to do likewise to those who are baptized. Just before ascending back to heaven, the Lord confers His power upon the twelve disciples, one by one, by the laying on of hands. (See Moroni 2:1-3.)

It is immediately noised abroad amongst the people that Jesus has appeared and will show Himself again on the morrow. Many people labor all night to come to the place where He will appear.

The next day, the disciples minister to the multitude as they have been instructed to do by Jesus. Then the twelve go down into the water and are baptized and filled with the Holy Ghost. Jesus visits the people again and teaches them for a three-day period. After that, He continues to visit them on occasion.

The disciples go forth teaching and baptizing. Those who are baptized receive the Holy Ghost and are numbered amongst the Church. The Church meets together often.

Because of disputations amongst the people concerning the name of the Church, the disciples gather together and unite in mighty prayer and fasting. Jesus appears to them and explains that the Church shall be called in His name and must be built upon His gospel.

Gospel Principles:

1. **Authority.** Jesus gave the twelve disciples the power to baptize (Aaronic priesthood) and the power to give the Holy Ghost (Melchizedek priesthood). (See 3 Nephi 11:21-22; 18:36-37.)

2. **Baptism.** Over the ages, the mode of baptism has been a subject for disagreement. It is an ordinance so important, as here emphasized by the Savior, that Satan is very interested in perverting it. (See 3 Nephi 11:22-30 and 33-34.)

3. **Church government.** The Savior gave specific instructions on how His church should be run: meet together often, forbid

not the unworthy to come, pray, fast, minister to the unworthy, administer the ordinances of sacrament and baptism, and call the Church and do all in His name. The disciples carried out His instructions. (See 3 Nephi 18:22-23 and 28-32; 19:5-8; 26:19-21; 27:3-8; Moroni 6:1-9.)

4. **Contention.** The father of contention, the Devil, tries to split the Church apart in all ages by driving in wedges of disputation about doctrine and ordinances. (See 3 Nephi 11:28-30; 18:34; 27:3-4.)

5. **Gospel of Jesus Christ.** The author of the gospel defined it in person: through faith, repentance, baptism, reception of the Holy Ghost, enduring to the end, and the power of Christ's atonement, we can be lifted up and enter into the Father's kingdom. (See 3 Nephi 27:10-22.)

6. **Holy Ghost.** Church meetings were conducted under the guidance and power of the third member of the Godhead. (See Moroni 6:9.)

7. **One, Importance of the.** Jesus took the time to let each person come forth and feel His wounds. (See 3 Nephi 11:15.)

8. **Prayer.** The Savior taught the people the importance and uses of prayer. (See 3 Nephi 18:15-23.)

9. **Sacrament.** Our reverence for this holy ordinance could be increased by imagining ourselves at the feet of the Redeemer, as these people were. (See 3 Nephi 18:2-11 and 28-30.)

10. **Sacrifice.** Many people struggled all night to come hear Jesus. (See 3 Nephi 19:3.) In modern days, many faithful saints sacrifice much to travel to the temples.

11. **Teaching.** The master teacher demonstrated the importance of repetition: He told them three times what His doctrine is. (See 3 Nephi 11:31-40.)

12. **Testimony.** Those who went forth and felt the wounds in Jesus' body had firsthand knowledge of His divinity. But, more blessed are those who believe without the advantage of touching and seeing. (See 3 Nephi 11:15; 12:2.)

13. **Witnesses.** This multitude of witnesses, who saw Christ, let their testimonies shine bright, unto the convincing of the people for four hundred years. Even today, we can still benefit from their marvelous experience. (See 3 Nephi 11:14-16; 12:2.)

* * *

STORY 67

JESUS BLESSES THE NEPHITE PEOPLE

Reference: 3 Nephi 17:1-25; 18:39; 19:1-4 and 13-36; 20:1-9; 26:13-16

Background: *As prophesied, Jesus Christ appeared to the Nephites after His resurrection. (See Story 65.) The multitude felt His wounds and witnessed that He was the Redeemer. He gave twelve disciples authority to baptize. The Sermon on the Mount and other teachings were delivered by Jesus. (See Story 66.)*

Story Outline: The Lord is ready to leave the people to ponder His words until the morrow, but He perceives that they would have Him tarry. Full of compassion, He calls forward the sick and afflicted and heals them.

Then Jesus gathers around Him all their little children. Kneeling in the midst of them, He prays unspeakable words to the Father in behalf of the multitude, who, also kneeling, are overcome with joy. He blesses the children one by one. Angels come down from heaven and encircle the children about with fire and minister unto them.

After administering the sacrament to the multitude, Jesus ascends into heaven. The people return to their homes and spread the news throughout the land. Many travel all night to come see and hear the Savior the next day. (See Story 66.)

On the morrow, the disciples minister to and teach the multitude. Then, at their baptism, the disciples receive the Holy Ghost. The multitude witnesses that the twelve are encircled as if by fire and that angels from heaven minister unto them. Jesus appears and also ministers unto the disciples. The disciples pray to Him and He prays to the Father for them. The multitude hears the marvelous words and sees that the disciples are as white as the countenance of the Lord.

Jesus provides bread and wine and administers the sacrament to the disciples, who then give it unto the multitude. He continues teaching the people many things over a period of three days. The tongues of the children are loosed by Jesus, and marvelous things are uttered. He ascends into heaven again, but appears often after that to break and bless bread with them.

Gospel Principles:

1. **Angels, Ministering of.** The glory of the angels was described as the brightness of fire. The duty of the angels was to minister to the children and to the disciples. (See 3 Nephi 17:24-25; 19:14-15.)

2. **Compassion.** The Savior really demonstrated His love and concern for the people. (See 3 Nephi 17:2-3 and 5-8.)

3. **Faith.** Greater blessings and miracles are given to those with greater faith. (See 3 Nephi 17:8-9; 19:35-36.)

4. **Jesus Christ.** From this story we get a unique account of our Savior's traits. We see His compassion, His love, His sorrow. We see Him spending time with the people, healing the sick, blessing the children individually, and praying with and for the disciples. And by the Spirit, we can get a taste of the joy that comes from being in His presence.

5. **Joy.** The joy of being in the presence of the Lord is indescribable and incomprehensible. The Savior's joy was also full on this wonderful occasion, insomuch that He wept. (See 3 Nephi 17:17-21.)

6. **One, Importance of the.** Though Jesus had other places to visit, He took the time to bless the children, one by one. These were of the rising generation, which would remain righteous and spread the testimony of His resurrection. (See 3 Nephi 17:4-6, 21 and 25.)

7. **Pondering.** We need to take time to ponder religious teachings so that the truth can sink into our hearts and revelation can be received. (See 3 Nephi 17:2-3.)

8. **Prayer.** Much of the time during the Lord's visit was spent in prayer. Through prayer and faith, the Holy Ghost came. The disciples were given the words they should pray through inspiration. Many people were praying at once, but all were heard. Have you ever felt the Lord's countenance smile upon you while you were praying? We, too, should follow the commandment not to cease praying in our hearts. (See 3 Nephi 17:13-18; 19:16-36; 20:1.)

9. **Revelation.** Great and marvelous things were uttered "out of the mouth of babes and sucklings." (See 3 Nephi 26:14 and 16; Matthew 21:16.) Little children are dear and close to Christ.

10. **Reverence.** In the presence of the Lord, it was natural to be reverent. (See 3 Nephi 17:10.) In our church meetings, we can feel His presence more when we show reverence.

11. **Sacrament.** During the sacrament, we should receive spiritual renewal. (See 3 Nephi 20:3-9.) The Savior administered the sacrament to the people often. (See 3 Nephi 26:13.)

12. **Sacrifice.** Many people struggled all night to come hear Jesus. (See 3 Nephi 19:3.) In modern days, many faithful saints sacrifice much to travel to the temples.

* * *

STORY 68

JESUS CORRECTS THE RECORDS

Reference: 3 Nephi 23:4-14; 24:1; 26:1-2; 27:23-26

Background: *After His resurrection, Jesus Christ visited the Nephite people who survived the great destruction. (See Story 65.) He chose twelve disciples and gave them authority to baptize and to govern the Church. (See Story 66.) During His visits, He healed the sick, blessed the children, and taught the people many things. (See Story 67.)*

Story Outline: After quoting and expounding the prophecies of Isaiah, the Savior gives a commandment to heed His words. He tells Nephi to write those things that He has told the people.

At the Lord's request, Nephi brings the records forward. Jesus points out that it was not recorded that many of the saints rose from the dead and appeared unto many at His resurrection. Upon the Savior's command, this missing fact is written into the records.

Jesus then relates some of the revelations given to Malachi and commands that the words be written. He expounds these scriptures unto the multitude.

At a later time, Jesus appears to the disciples and commands them to write the things that they have seen and heard and the works of the people, for out of the books shall the world be judged.

<u>Gospel Principles:</u>

1. **Journals.** The Savior's injunction gives us some guidelines for what to write in our journals: things we have seen and heard and works of the people. We will be judged out of the books that are kept. (See 3 Nephi 27:23-26.)

2. **Judgement.** Two sets of books, one on earth, one in heaven, will be used in the final judgement. (See 3 Nephi 27:25-26.)

3. **Prophecy.** It is important for us to know that the words of the Lord through His prophets are fulfilled. (See 3 Nephi 23:9-13.)

4. **Prophets.** The author of the scriptures made sure that they were properly written. He is familiar with all of the prophets in all parts of the world in all time periods, Samuel the Lamanite, Malachi, Isaiah, etc. (See 3 Nephi 23:1 and 9; 24:1; 26:2.)

5. **Records.** It is important to the Lord that the records are complete and accurate. (See 3 Nephi 23:4 and 6-13; 26:2; 27:23-26.)

6. **Resurrection.** Christ was the first fruit of the resurrection, but in the new world, as well as in the old, many saints also arose. (See 3 Nephi 23:9-10.)

7. **Scriptures.** The scriptures were recorded for future generations, for our benefit. (See 3 Nephi 23:4-6; 26:2.)

8. **Teaching.** Jesus taught by expounding the scriptures. (See 3 Nephi 23:14; 26:1.)

9. **Witnesses.** Because the Savior corrected the records, we have the testimony of those who witnessed the resurrection of many saints after He arose. (See 3 Nephi 23:9-13.)

* * *

STORY 69

THE EFFECT OF CHRIST'S VISIT LASTS TWO HUNDRED YEARS

Reference: 4 Nephi 1:1-49

Background: *Jesus Christ visited the Nephites after His resurrection. He taught them many things, blessed them, ordained twelve disciples, set up His church, corrected their records, and expounded the scriptures to them. (See Stories 65 through 68.)*

Story Outline: The disciples spread the gospel and establish the Church throughout the land. Within a few years, all of the people are converted and baptized.

Peace reigns, and the people have possessions in common. The disciples work great miracles. Destroyed cities are rebuilt as the people of Nephi prosper, multiply, and spread out upon the land.

The first generation from Christ and most of the second generation pass away without having any contentions. The love of God abounds in people's hearts.

After two hundred years, the Nephite people begin to be lifted up in pride. No longer having things in common, they divide up into classes. Again, the Lamanite name is used. Churches other than the true one are formed. Contentions arise and, eventually, the secret Gadianton oaths are built up again.

By 300 A. D., the Lamanites and the Nephites are exceedingly wicked. Gadianton robbers are spread over all the land. In 321 A.D., Ammaron, keeper of the plates, is constrained by the Holy Ghost to hide up the sacred records.

Gospel Principles:

1. **Church government.** As the original twelve disciples passed away, others were ordained in their steads to maintain a quorum of twelve. (See v. 14.)

2. **Deception.** Counterfeit is one of Satan's chief tools. Many were led astray by false churches, "having a form of godliness, but denying the power thereof." (See v. 26-28; 2 Timothy 3:5.) Others were blinded to the truth. (See v. 26-34.)

3. **Example.** In performing miracles, the disciples were doing what they saw Jesus do. (See v. 5; 3 Nephi 27:21.)

4. **Generation gap.** Where does the passing on of testimony to posterity break down? (See v. 22-24.)

5. **Joy.** With the love of God in their hearts, the people experienced the joy of living in peace with each other. (See v. 15-18.)

6. **Love.** Love of God and fellow man brought peace to the Nephites to the extent that they could share possessions. (See v. 2-3 and 15-18.)

7. **Peace.** For two hundred years, the Nephites experienced the utopia that comes from truly living the gospel. This heavenly gift, the longest period of peace in the history of the world, was ushered in by the Prince of Peace. (See v. 2-3 and 15-18.)

8. **Pearls before swine.** The precious sacred records were taken out of the midst of the people when they became so wicked. (See v. 48-49.)

9. **Pride.** It was pride that brought to an end the unprecedented period of peace, joy, and love. (See v. 23-26 and 43-45.)

10. **Riches.** The people could not handle their prosperity in Christ. Pride and selfishness crept in and grew like cancer. (See v. 23-26.)

11. **Steadfastness.** The period of peace did not come as a blessing without effort. The saints prayed, fasted, met together often, and kept the commandments. (See v. 2-3 and 12.)

12. **Unity.** Having possessions in common is an ultimate test of charity and unity. The people of Nephi passed the test for two hundred years before pride took its toll. (See v. 3 and 15.)

* * *

STORY 70

MORMON AND MORONI WITNESS THE FINAL DESTRUCTION OF THE NEPHITES

Reference: Mormon 1:1-19; 2:1-29; 3:1-16; 4:1-23; 5:1-9; 6:1-22; 8:1-14; Moroni 1:1-4; 8:27-30; 9:1-26; 10:1-2

Background: *About three hundred years after Christ's visit, the Nephites and the Lamanites became so wicked that Ammaron, the keeper of the plates, was constrained by the Holy Ghost to hide up the sacred records. (See Story 69.)*

Story Outline: Ammaron charges Mormon, then a boy of ten, to observe the people and, at age twenty-four, to write their proceedings on the plates of Nephi.

Mormon chronicles alternating years of bloodshed and peace. The land is covered with buildings and multitudes of people. Wickedness prevails and miracles cease. The three disciples who had tarried on the earth and the Holy Ghost are withdrawn. Because of the hardness of the hearts of the people, Mormon is forbidden to preach.

At age fifteen, Mormon is appointed to be the leader of the Nephite armies to battle against the Lamanites. Revolution and carnage spread throughout the land. The Nephites are full of sorrow but not unto repentance. They no longer have the strength of the Lord with them in their battles.

For ten years, a treaty keeps peace between the Nephites in the land northward and the Lamanites in the south. Mormon preaches repentance and baptism but is rejected because of hardened hearts.

The Lamanites again declare war but are repulsed by the Nephite armies under Mormon's leadership. Encouraged by their success, the Nephites boast their own strength and swear to take revenge upon their enemies. As directed by the Lord, Mormon refuses to lead them in their wicked desire. Thousands on both sides perish as battles are successively won and lost in the land of Desolation.

As years pass, the Lamanites eventually gain the greater advantage. Mormon consents to lead the Nephite armies again. But, because the people will not repent, they are driven and swept off before their enemies.

Mormon writes to his son, Moroni, telling of the horrible scenes of wickedness: rape, torture, and cannibalism. He puts the care of the sacred records into the hands of Moroni.

The Nephites gather themselves together in one body around the hill Cumorah for their final struggle. The Lamanite armies fall upon them, destroying twenty-three groups of ten thousand people each. Only twenty-four Nephite survivors remain alive, including Mormon and Moroni. Mormon laments over his fallen people.

Moroni finishes the records of his father. (See Story 80.) Mormon and the others of the twenty-four are hunted down and slain. Moroni alone remains, the last Nephite unwilling to deny the Christ. For over twenty years, he wanders where he can to protect his life, adding to the records, as he can, those things that he hopes will be of worth to us. In 421 A. D., he seals the plates and hides them up unto the Lord.

Gospel Principles:

1. **Anger.** Anger is a tool of Satan. It devours brotherly love. (See Moroni 9:3-5.)

2. **Charity.** After watching his enemies kill all of his friends, relatives, and countrymen, Moroni still had charity enough to call the Lamanites his brethren and to write things that might be of worth to them. What a divine attribute is charity. (See Moroni 1:4; 10:1.)

3. **Chastity.** Modern society subtly robs women of their modesty and virtue through advertising, entertainment, and pornography. Chastity is not considered sacred and precious in the media of today's world. (See Moroni 9:9-10; Jacob 2:28.)

4. **Courage.** Moroni refused to deny Christ, though it put his life in peril. (See Moroni 1:2-3.)

5. **Diligence.** Even though it was for an apparent lost cause, Mormon and Moroni continued to labor. (See Moroni 9:6.)

6. **Enduring.** Mormon and Moroni held to their beliefs until the end, while others were falling all around them. (See Mormon 2:19; 8:4-5; Moroni 1:2-3.)

7. **Fear.** Fear, devoid of all hope, filled the breasts of the wicked Nephites. They were alone, without God, unprepared for victory, and unprepared for death, facing destruction. (See Mormon 6:7-8; *D&C* 38:30.)

8. **Hardheartedness.** Hardened hearts were closed against the promptings and healing influence of the Spirit. The Nephites allowed their callousness to increase, thereby denying themselves blessings from God. (See Mormon 1:16-17; 4:11-12; Moroni 9:4.)

9. **Obedience.** Mormon and Moroni faithfully fulfilled the commandments they were given, whether it was to preach or refrain from preaching or to write or refrain from writing. (See Mormon 1:16-17; 3:2-3; 5:8-9; 8:3-4.)

10. **Pearls before swine.** Look at all the blessings that were taken away from the Nephites. They were too wicked to have the Holy Ghost, the gifts of the Spirit, the ministry of the three disciples, and the preaching of the gospel. They were even denied the leadership of their righteous general. (See Mormon 1:13-18; 3:9-16; 8:10.)

11. **Preparation.** Under Mormon's counsel, the Nephites prepared physically for battle. But, they refused to prepare spiritually. Thus, they denied themselves the greater protection. (See Mormon 3:1-3.)

12. **Pride.** Mormon attributed the downfall of the entire Nephite nation to pride. (See Moroni 8:27; D&C 38:39.)

13. **Reward for wickedness.** We cannot escape the judgements of God. The Hardheartedness of the Nephites was the cause of their own suffering. (See Mormon 1:17-19; 4:4-5 and 11-12.)

14. **Sorrow.** The sorrow of the Nephites in their trials was not of the godly type, which worketh repentance (2 Corinthians 7:10). It was the sorrow of the damned. (See Mormon 2:10-14.)

15. **Steadfastness.** What a bleak sojourn in life was the lot of Moroni. He spent twenty years as a lone fugitive, yet, still remained true to the end. (See Moroni 1:3.)

16. **Vengeance.** The Lord reserves vengeance unto Himself. The Nephites entered on the path of destruction when they sought after revenge. (See Mormon 3:14-16; 4:4-5.)

17. **Youth.** Mormon was an outstanding young man. He was given the charge to keep the records when he was only ten. At age fifteen, he was visited of the Lord and was also appointed to be the leader of the Nephite armies. (See Mormon 1:2-3 and 15; 2:1-2.)

* * *

STORY 71

THE HISTORY OF THE JAREDITE NATION IS REVEALED

Reference: Omni 1:20-23 and 27-30; Mosiah 28:10-20; Ether 1:1-2

Background: *Mosiah was warned by the Lord to leave the land of Nephi and take with him those who would hearken unto the Lord. They discovered the land of Zarahemla, which was peopled by the Mulekites. Mosiah was appointed king over the two groups of people. (See Story 16.)*

Story Outline: King Mosiah interprets the engravings on a large stone that is brought to him in Zarahemla. They tell of the fallen nation of the Jaredites and the lone surviving man, Coriantumr.

Coriantumr is discovered by the people of Zarahemla. He lives with them for nine moons before passing away. (See Stories 78 and 79.)

Amaleki, born in the days of Mosiah, lives to see the throne passed on to Mosiah's son, Benjamin. Amaleki records the story of some people who return to the land of Nephi, namely Zeniff and his followers. (See Story 21.)

Zeniff becomes king over the people in the land of Nephi. As the years go by, the kingdom there passes from father to son, from Zeniff to Noah to Limhi.

King Limhi sends men out to find Zarahemla. Instead, they find the ruins of the Jaredite nation and twenty-four gold plates, which they cannot read. (See Story 27.)

Meanwhile, in Zarahemla, the kingdom passes from Mosiah to Benjamin and then to Benjamin's son, Mosiah. During this second Mosiah's reign, Ammon is sent to the land of Nephi, where he finds Limhi and his people. King Limhi is anxious to have the contents of the twenty-four gold plates interpreted and is filled with joy to learn that King Mosiah has the power to translate. (See Stories 20 and 27.)

Limhi brings the twenty-four plates to King Mosiah who then translates them using seer stones. (See Story 32.) The plates are a record of the Jaredites from the time they came to this land from the tower of Babel until the entire nation was destroyed, except for Coriantumr. Their account, as taken from the twenty-four plates, is given in the Book of Ether. (See Stories 72 through 79.)

Gospel Principles:

1. **Forgetfulness.** Will we learn from the histories of two previous civilizations that were destroyed because of pride and wickedness? Or will we forget and make the same mistakes?

2. **Gifts of the Spirit.** The gift of translation is given of God for the benefit of all men, so that we can learn and repent. (See Omni 1:20; Mosiah 28:11-16.)

3. **Knowledge.** Limhi's people were extremely curious to know about the destroyed nation that they discovered, and they were grateful for the knowledge. In the long run, that knowledge did

not benefit the Nephites. They eventually succumbed to the same fate as the Jaredites. (See Mosiah 28:12 and 17-18.)

4. **Records.** We know about the Jaredite nation from four sources:
    a) The stone that was found,
    b) The bones and ruins in the land northward,
    c) The witness of the lone survivor, Coriantumr, and
    d) The twenty-four gold plates.

    The Lord made sure that the record of these people was preserved and revealed for our benefit. (See Mosiah 28:13-15 and 18-20.)

5. **Scriptures.** We can learn from the mistakes of others by studying and applying the scriptures.

6. **Teaching.** The Lord wants us to know about the Jaredites, their iniquities and abominations. He teaches us through revealing scriptures to us.

* * *

STORY 72

JARED AND HIS FAMILY ARE NOT CONFOUNDED

<u>Reference</u>: Ether 1:33-43

<u>Background</u>: *The history of the Jaredites was translated by King Mosiah from the twenty-four gold plates found by the people of Limhi. (See Story 71.) Moroni made an account of the history in the Book of Ether. (See Ether 1:1-3.) Jared and his family lived at the time of the great tower of Babel, when God confounded the language of the people and scattered them.*

<u>Story Outline</u>: Jared asks his brother to cry unto the Lord that the two of them may not have their language confounded so that they can still understand each other. The Lord has compassion and grants their request.

Then, Jared asks his brother to approach the Lord on behalf of their friends and their families. Again, the Lord has compassion and does not confound their language.

Next, Jared asks his brother to cry unto the Lord to inquire whither they will be driven, that perhaps it might be to a choice land, if they are faithful. The Lord is mindful of the long time that the brother of Jared prays and answers with a promise to lead them to a land choice above all the lands of the earth. The Lord gives instructions for Jared and his brother with their friends and all of their families to gather together, taking provisions with them.

The brother of Jared is promised that a very great nation shall come from the descendants of these people.

Gospel Principles:

1. **Communication.** Without common language, people are divided. Sometimes people in the same family don't "speak the same language."

2. **Faith.** Both Jared and his brother asked in faith.

3. **Family.** It was important to Jared and his brother to keep their families together. They realized that the Lord was the key for doing so.

4. **Generation gap.** Breakdown of communications is a sure way to break up families.

5. **Gifts of the Spirit.** Jared recognized that his brother was favored of the Lord, that he could petition the Lord and receive revelation. (See v. 34-35 and 39-40.)

6. **Prayer.**
    *   Jared was inspired to know what to ask for. (See v. 38.) We need to be in tune with the Spirit because God knows what we need before we ask for it.
    *   Obtaining answers to prayers requires effort. The brother of Jared had to cry unto the Lord for a long time. Then, the Lord rewarded that effort. (See v. 43.)

7. **Prophecy.** The stories that follow will show that the Lord fulfills His word as revealed through His prophets. (See v. 42-43.)

David S. Taylor

8. **Reward for righteousness.** What a blessing it was for Jared with his relatives and friends not to have their language confounded. Not only that, but because of their faithfulness, they were led to a choice land where their posterity became a great nation. (See v. 35-38 and 42-43.)

* * *

236

STORY 73

THE BROTHER OF JARED FORGETS TO PRAY

Reference: Ether 2:1-8 and 13-15

Background: *Through prayer and faith, Jared and his brother, with their families and friends, did not have their language confounded at the tower of Babel. They obtained a promise from the Lord that they would be led to a choice land. (See Story 72.)*

Story Outline: Jared and all those associated with him go down into the valley of Nimrod, taking with them provisions of all kinds: flocks, fish, bees, and seeds. From within a cloud, the Lord talks to the brother of Jared, giving him directions where the group should travel into the wilderness.

As guided by the Lord through the wilderness, the people have to build barges to cross many waters. Finally, they arrive at the great sea and pitch their tents on the seashore.

After they dwell on the seashore for four years, the Lord again visits the brother of Jared, speaking from within a cloud. The Lord talks with him for three hours and chastens him for not remembering to pray. The brother of Jared repents and calls upon the Lord for his brethren. The Lord forgives him and admonishes him and his people to sin no more.

Gospel Principles:

1. **Enduring.** Even a prophet, one with whom the Lord has personally spoken, needs to remain diligent and faithful. We must not ever neglect prayer or any of our other religious duties.

2. **Forgetfulness.** Why do we not remember to call upon the Lord? When things are going well, it seems that we do not turn to Him. Here was a man, to whom the Lord had spoken, who forgot to say his prayers during a period of four years. (See v. 13-14.)

3. **Prayer.** We can see how great an importance the Lord places on prayer by how he chastened the brother of Jared. (See v. 14.)

4. **Preparation.** The food storage of these people even included fish and honey bees. (See v. 1-3.)

5. **Repentance.** There is a pattern for repentance in this story: chastisement, repentance, prayer, forgiveness, sinning no more. (See v. 14-15.)

6. **Reward for righteousness.** The promised land was preserved for a righteous people who would serve God or else be swept off. (See v. 7-8.)

* * *

STORY 74

THE BROTHER OF JARED SEES THE FINGER OF THE LORD

Reference: Ether 2:16-25; 3:1-28

Background: *Jared and his brother with their friends and families were led by the Lord from the tower of Babel through the wilderness to the seashore, where they dwelt for four years. (See Story 73.)*

Story Outline: The Lord tells the brother of Jared to go to work and build some barges. As made according to the Lord's directions, the barges are watertight on top, sides, and bottom.

The brother of Jared asks the Lord how the people are to breathe and see while inside the vessels. For breathing, the brother of Jared is told to make stopped holes, one in the top and one in the bottom, to receive air into the ships. However, concerning light for seeing, he is not given the answer. Instead, the Lord turns the problem back to him.

The brother of Jared goes into mount Shelem and moltens out of rock sixteen small stones, two for each of the eight barges. On the top of the mount, he sets out the stones and prays with great faith that the Lord will touch them with His finger and cause them to give off light for the journey.

The Lord does touch the stones with His finger. The veil is lifted and the brother of Jared sees the finger of the Lord. He falls down in fear. The Lord asks him if he saw more than His finger. The brother of Jared answers, "Nay; Lord, show thyself unto me."

Because of the great faith of the brother of Jared, the Lord, Jesus Christ, shows Himself and explains His pre-mortal spirit body. The Lord teaches him and ministers unto him, showing him all the inhabitants of the earth from the beginning to the end of time. The brother of Jared is told to write and seal up the things that he has seen, along with a means for interpretation, to come forth at a later time.

Gospel Principles:

1. **Faith.** Read the brother of Jared's faithful prayer. The Lord, Himself, declared the brother of Jared to be a prime example of one who has faith. (See Ether 3:2-5, 9 and 26.)

2. **Gifts of the Spirit.** The things revealed to the brother of Jared were to be protected and revealed later by the gift of the interpretation of tongues. (See Ether 3:22-24.)

3. **Godhead.** What a clear lesson of the nature of God and man is taught to the brother of Jared by the Savior! Jesus is the God of the *Old Testament.* Man is created in God's image. Jesus' spiritual body looked like His physical body that He would take upon Himself when He came to dwell upon the earth. (See Ether 3:6-10 and 15-16.)

4. **Jesus Christ.**
   - The brother of Jared sought for light: irradiant stones for lamps. He found the source of eternal light, the Redeemer.
   - If we receive Christ, we will become His sons and daughters. (See Ether 3:14.)

5. **Knowledge.** The faith of the brother of Jared turned into perfect knowledge as he saw the Lord. (See Ether 3:19-20.)

6. **Obedience.** The brother of Jared did all that the Lord commanded him to do. (See Ether 2:16-18 and 21-22.)

7. **Prayer.** Pray like everything depends upon the Lord and work like everything depends on you. (See Ether 2:22; 3:1-2.)

8. **Preparation.** How can we prepare for the mountain waves of life that will crash upon us? (See Ether 2:24-25.)

9. **Self-reliance.** We are not given all the answers. We must first study out problems on our own, and then approach God. (See Ether 2:23; *D&C* 9:7-9.)

10. **Teaching.** The Lord had previously instructed Jared's party and had let them practice making barges. (See Story 73 and Ether 2:16.)

11. **Work.** "Go to work and build," was the instruction from the Lord. (See Ether 2:16.) The same command could well be applied to us in our callings to serve others.

* * *

STORY 75

THE JAREDITES CROSS THE SEA TO THE PROMISED LAND

<u>Reference</u>: Ether 6:1-30

<u>Background</u>: *Led by the Lord from the tower of Babel through the wilderness to the seashore, Jared and his brother with their friends and families built eight, water-tight barges to cross the sea. Desiring to have light in the boats, the brother of Jared prepared sixteen stones, prayed, and witnessed the Lord touching the stones with His finger to make them give off light. (See Story 74.)*

<u>Story Outline</u>: The sixteen stones are placed in the eight vessels to give light for the journey across the sea. Animals, provisions, and people are loaded into the barges.

The Jaredites commend themselves to God upon the waters. The Lord causes a furious wind to blow their boats across the sea to the promised land. The families sing praises to the Lord as they go. When they arrive on the shore of the promised land, they bow down in humility and shed tears of joy.

The Jaredites till the earth and multiply and spread upon their new land. They are taught to walk humbly before the Lord.

In their old age, Jared and his brother gather their families together. The descendants desire to have a king appointed over them. Though the idea is grievous to the two patriarchs, they indulge their offspring. However, all of their sons but one refuse to be king.

Orihah, the son of Jared, is anointed to be king. He reigns in righteousness, remembering the goodness and greatness of the Lord. Jared and his brother both pass away.

Gospel Principles:

1. **Divine guidance.** The wind never ceased to blow the Jaredites across the water toward the promised land. Even so, the Holy Spirit will always guide us to eternal life. We just have to stay in the current. (See v. 8.)

2. **Faith.**
   - It took faith by the Jaredites to commend themselves unto the Lord upon the waters for 344 days. (See v. 4 and 11.)
   - By faith and prayer, their boats were brought to the surface when buried in the depths of the waters. (See v. 7.)

3. **Family home evening.** It sounds like the brother of Jared held family home evening daily, singing and praising the Lord. (See v. 9.)

4. **Gratitude.** It is amazing that the people of Jared maintained an attitude of gratitude all throughout their long voyage upon the waters. (See v. 9-12.)

5. **Humility.** Because the Jaredites realized what the Lord had done for them, they were humble. (See v. 12 and 17.)

6. **Industry.** That the Jaredites were industrious is evident. They prepared well for their voyage, and when they arrived in the promised land, they set to work. (See v. 4 and 13.)

7. **Joy.** Counting our blessings makes us humble and grateful and gives us joy. (See v. 12.)

8. **Mercy.** The Lord was merciful to Jared and his people, not only in allowing their language not to be confounded, but also, in leading them to a promised land. (See v. 12.)

9. **Prayer.** When we are encompassed about by waters of temptation or discouragement, prayer is the tool to bring us to the top again. (See v. 7.)

10. **Preparation.** Because the Jaredites had prepared well, they did not suffer on their long voyage. (See v. 2-4 and 9-11.)

11. **Teaching.** Are we not "taught from on high" when we listen to the Spirit? (See v. 17.)

12. **Trust in God.** After all the preparation they had done, the Jaredites still had to put their trust in the Lord to take them safely to the promised land. (See v. 4-8.)

* * *

STORY 76

JAREDITE KINGS VIE FOR POWER

Reference: Ether 7:1-27; 8:1-19; 9:1-22

Background: *Jared and his brother with their friends and families were led by the Lord from the tower of Babel into the wilderness and then across the sea to the promised land. Before they died, the two brothers, against their wishes, appointed a king at the request of their growing posterity. The brother of Jared warned them that having a king would lead to captivity. (See Story 75 and Ether 6:21-24.)*

Story Outline: Orihah, the first Jaredite king, reigns in righteousness. The throne then passes to his son, Kib. Kib's reign is interrupted by a rebellion led by his son Corihor. Kib is placed in captivity by his son, where he begets Shule.

Shule grows in strength and judgement. He takes the throne away from his brother, Corihor, and restores it to his father, Kib. As a reward, Kib passes the kingdom on to Shule.

Though Corihor repents and is given power in the kingdom, one of his sons, Noah, rebels against King Shule, taking the King into captivity. Shule's sons, in turn, slay Noah and free their father.

Two kingdoms develop, one of Shule and one of Noah's son, Cohor. Cohor gives battle unto Shule and is slain. Cohor's son, Nimrod, gives his father's kingdom over to Shule. Prophets preach and bring the people unto repentance. The remainder of Shule's reign is peaceful and righteous.

Shule's son, Omer, is appointed king to reign in his father's stead. Jared, son of Omer, rebels. Flattering half of the kingdom to follow him, Jared overthrows his father and keeps him in captivity for half of his life. Two other of Omer's sons take back the kingdom for their father.

Jared regrets losing the kingdom. To get it back for him, his daughter brings up the secret oaths and dances before Akish for Omer's head. Akish gathers his kinsfolk and administers the secret oaths to them.

Omer's kingdom is overthrown because of the secret combinations of Akish. But, the Lord warns Omer in a dream so that he and his family depart in safety. Jared reigns and gives his dancer daughter to be the wife of Akish.

Akish, using the secret combinations, murders his father-in-law, Jared, on the throne and takes over as king. Akish is jealous of one of his sons and starves him to death. Another son of Akish, Nimrah, escapes with a small band and joins Omer in his exile.

Other sons of Akish draw away followers and make war with their father. In the war between Akish and his sons, which lasts many years, all but thirty people are destroyed.

Omer brings his people back and is once again established as king. Being old, he anoints his son, Emer, to reign in his stead. Under Emer's righteous reign, the kingdom prospers.

Gospel Principles:

1. **Appearance.** Fair outward appearance can be deceiving. Look to the heart for the truth. (See Ether 7:4; 8:10.)

2. **Divine guidance.** By following the warning from the Lord, Omer saved the lives of himself and his family. (See Ether 9:3.) Has the Lord given us any warnings to save our eternal lives?

3. **Honoring parents.** In the striving for power in this story, we see extremes of parental honor and lack of it: rebellion, captivity, revenge, and restoration. (See Ether 7:4, 7-9, 15 and 18; 8:3.)

4. **Law.** Law should bring about good for the people. In our times, perhaps Shule's law would be opposed as being discriminatory. (See Ether 7:25.)

5. **Persecution.** In all ages, there are those who mock and revile the prophets. (See Ether 7:24.)

6. **Prophets.** The prophets were sent to warn the people and call them to repentance. Because the people heeded the word, they were blessed instead of cursed. (See Ether 7:23-26.)

7. **Remembrance.** By attending church meetings, partaking of the sacrament, and studying the scriptures, can we remember what God has done for us to the extent that we will live righteously? (See Ether 7:27.)

8. **Repentance.** Shule's people were spared because they repented. (See Ether 7:25-26.)

9. **Reward for wickedness.** Those who set up the secret combinations to murder for gain were caught and destroyed in their own web. (See Ether 9:4-7 and 12.)

10. **Scriptures.** Jared's daughter was so devious that she used the records for an evil purpose. (See Ether 8:9.)

11. **Unrighteous dominion.** Desire for power and kingdoms brought captivity and murder. (See Ether 7:5.)

12. **Worldliness.** Concern for the things of this world, power, affluence, and glory, were the corrupting factors that brought about great evil and suffering. (See Ether 8:7; 9:11.)

* * *

STORY 77

THE JAREDITES PASS THROUGH CYCLES OF GOOD AND EVIL

<u>Reference</u>: Ether 9:21-35; 10:1-34; 11:1-23

<u>Background</u>: *Government by kings brought about greed, captivity, murder, and secret combinations amongst the Jaredite nation in the promised land. (See Story 76.)*

<u>Story Outline</u>: King Emer reigns in peace and righteousness as does his son Coriantum. The son of Coriantum, Com, in turn, rules as king for forty-nine years. Com is slain by his own son, Heth, who then takes over as king. Because of the wickedness and secret plans in the land, prophets come, crying repentance. The prophets are ill-treated by the command of King Heth. As prophesied by the prophets, the land is cursed with dearth and poisonous serpents. Heth and many others perish. The people, seeing that they must also perish, begin to repent. Shez, a descendant of Heth, builds up the broken people into a righteous kingdom.

The kingdom passes from Shez to his son, Riplakish, who uses his power to oppress the people and get gain and glory for himself. After forty-two years of Riplakish's wicked and burdensome reign, the people rise up in rebellion, kill the King, and drive his leaders out of the land.

Many years later, Morianton, a descendant of Riplakish, gathers an army and gains power over many cities. He establishes himself as king and eases the burdens of the people. Though he reigns justly, his personal life is wicked. The kingdom prospers.

Morianton's son, Kim, succeeds to the throne, reigns wickedly, is deposed by his brother, and lives and dies in captivity. Kim's son, Levi, takes the throne to himself by war. Levi reigns in righteousness, as do his successors, Corom, Kish, and Lib. In the days of Lib, commerce expands and the people prosper exceedingly.

Lib begets Hearthom, who reigns in his father's stead for twenty-four years until the throne is taken away from him. Hearthom lives the rest of his days in captivity. Four more generations, Heth, Aaron, Amnigaddah, and Coriantum, dwell in captivity all their lives. Then Com, son of Coriantum, gains power over the kingdom through many years of battles. In the days of Com, there come robbers using the ancient, secret oaths. Prophets warn of total destruction if the people do not repent of their murders and wickedness. Rejected and hunted by the people, the prophets flee to Com for protection and prophesy many things to him.

Shiblon reigns in Com's stead. Shiblon's brother rebels, starts a great war, and puts to death the prophets who prophesy of the destruction of the Jaredites. Contentions, wars, famines, pestilence, and destruction increase greatly to the point that the people begin to repent. Shiblon is slain, and his son, Seth, is brought into captivity.

Ahah, son of Seth, obtains the kingdom and reigns in wickedness. Ethem and Moron also rule wickedly. A rebellion divides Moron's kingdom in two. Eventually, Moron is overthrown and spends the rest of his days in captivity. He begets Coriantor, who lives his whole life as a captive. In the days of Coriantor, many prophets, including his son, Ether, come and prophesy destruction except the people should repent. The words of the prophets are rejected because of the wickedness of the people and their secret combinations.

Gospel Principles:

1. **Example.** Generally, the people followed the pattern set by their king, whether righteous or evil.

2. **Jesus Christ.** Emer was righteous enough that he saw the Savior. (See Ether 9:22.)

3. **Leadership.** The examples in this story show the importance of choosing good leaders. Compare Riplakish and Levi, for instance. (See Ether 10:5-7 and 16.)

4. **Prophets.**
   • Several different times, prophets were sent by the Lord to warn the people to repent. As the people became more wicked, the warnings dealt with utter destruction of the Jaredite nation. (See Ether 9:28-30; 11:1-3, 5-7, 12-13 and 20-21.)
   • From our perspective, we can easily see that it would have been beneficial for the Jaredites to heed the prophets, for their prophecies came to pass. But, we have prophets on the earth today, do we not? Are we heeding their words for our benefit?

5. **Remembrance.** Shez built up a righteous kingdom because he remembered the Lord's dealings with his forefathers. Remembrance can be a key or guide in our own lives to bring steadiness in keeping the commandments. (See Ether 10:2.)

6. **Repentance.** It seems that conditions had to get severely threatening before the Jaredites would start to repent. (See Ether 9:34-35; 11:7-8.)

* * *

251

STORY 78

THE PROPHET ETHER
WITNESSES THE DESTRUCTION
OF THE JAREDITES

Reference: Ether 11:23; 12:1-6; 13:1-2 and 13-22; 15:1-6 and 29-34

Background: *The record of the Jaredite people on twenty-four gold plates told of a succession of kings, who reigned in cycles of righteousness and wickedness. Though warned by prophets at several different times to repent or be destroyed, the Jaredites continued to grow more wicked. (See Story 77.)*

Story Outline: The prophet, Ether, is born of Coriantor in captivity in the days of King Coriantumr. Driven by the Spirit, Ether goes forth, prophesying to the people, exhorting them to have faith and repent. His words are rejected. He is cast out and has to dwell in a cave during the day. At night, he comes out and views the destruction of his people resulting from a great war that arises, wherein secret combinations fight against the King. Ether keeps a record.

In the second year of the war, the Lord sends Ether to King Coriantumr to prophesy. Ether tells the King that if he and his household will not repent, none of the Jaredites but Coriantumr, himself, will be spared, and that he will be buried by another people who will inherit the promised land. Coriantumr refuses to repent, and the great war continues. Ether hides in the cave again to save his life.

It is not until more than two million of the Jaredites have been slain and Coriantumr, himself, is seriously wounded, that he begins to remember the words of Ether. He mourns and begins to repent. He tries to surrender to his opponent, Shiz, but his people are angered, and the battle continues.

Over a period of four years, both armies gather all the people in the land to fight, arming men, women, and children for the final conflict. Drunk with anger and blinded by Satan, the people refuse peace and press on day by day, in dwindling numbers, to destroy each other. Ether monitors and chronicles this great destruction. The struggle eventually comes down to the two kings as the only ones still living. In the end, Coriantumr smites off the head of Shiz and becomes the lone survivor of the Jaredite nation as Ether had prophesied.

Ether is commanded of the Lord to go forth. He finishes his record and hides it up until it is found by the people of Limhi. (See Story 71.)

Gospel Principles:

1. **Anger.** Anger, this strong emotion, blinded both of the warring sides to the possibilities and blessings of peace. (See Ether 15:4-6.)

2. **Diligence.** Ether labored diligently all the day long to do that which the Lord had commanded of him. (See Ether 12:2-3.)

3. **Faith.** The people to whom Ether preached lacked faith. They would not believe without seeing. (See Ether 12:5.)

4. **Holy Ghost.** The Spirit in Ether was so strong that he could not be restrained. (See Ether 12:2.)

5. **Prophecy.** The prophecies of Ether concerning the fate of Coriantumr came to pass completely: because he did not repent, Coriantumr became the sole survivor of the Jaredites. (See Ether 13:20-21; 15:1-3 and 30-33. Also, see Story 71.)

6. **Prophets.** Like many other prophets, Ether was not honored by the people. They rejected his words and even sought his life. In reality, it was the Lord, whose representative Ether was, that the people rejected. (See Ether 12:5; 13:13 and 22.)

7. **Records.** The record that Ether kept stands as a witness against the Jaredites and as a warning to us: heed the prophets and repent or be destroyed. (See Ether 13:14.)

8. **Repentance.** Oh, that Coriantumr and the others had repented! The destruction could have been avoided. Coriantumr left it until too late to try to stem the tide. (See Ether 13:17 and 20-22; 15:1-6.)

* * *

STORY 79

CORIANTUMR CHOOSES DESTRUCTION OVER REPENTANCE

Reference: Ether 12:1-3; 13:15-31; 14:1-31; 15:1-33; Omni 1:20-22

Background: *The Jaredites, though warned by prophets at several different times to repent or be destroyed, passed through cycles of righteousness and wickedness, but continued to grow more wicked. (See Story 77.)*

Story Outline: Coriantumr is king over all the land. Ether, a prophet of the Lord, warns the people to repent or be destroyed. (See Story 78.) Ether's words are rejected, and he is cast out.

Many mighty men rise up and seek to destroy King Coriantumr by using secret combinations. However, he is wise in the ways of the world and combats his enemies. Many die in the war for the throne.

Ether comes again and prophesies to Coriantumr that if he and his household will repent, his kingdom will be preserved and the people will be spared. Otherwise, the Jaredite nation will be utterly destroyed; only he, Coriantumr, will survive to see another people inherit the land. Coriantumr chooses not to repent, and the wars continue.

Coriantumr is defeated and captured by Shared. But the next year, Coriantumr's sons beat Shared and return the kingdom to their father. A state of anarchy develops with robbers and bands selfishly fighting against each other.

A great battle ensues between the armies of Coriantumr and of Shared. In great anger, the two forces fight ferociously for several days until Coriantumr finally slays Shared. A wound in Coriatumr's thigh keeps him off the battlefield for two years, but the bloodshed goes on throughout the whole land.

Gilead, the brother of Shared, battles against Coriantumr and is successful at taking over the throne. Both men build up their armies. Gilead uses secret combinations. Lib, the High Priest, turns on Gilead, slays him and ascends to the throne. Coriantumr defeats and slays Lib but is wounded again in the process. Shiz, the brother of Lib, takes over Lib's army and becomes a terror in the land, killing women and children and burning cities.

The people divide themselves into the two camps of Coriantumr and Shiz. The dead bodies from battle after battle lie unburied, causing a great stink in all the land. Coriantumr is wounded badly by Shiz. Millions have been slain. Coriantumr starts to remember Ether's prophecy. He tries to repent and call a truce, but Shiz will not accept the terms of peace. Driven by anger, the people on both sides return to battle.

For four years, all the surviving people in the land are gathered together to strengthen the two opposing armies. Men, women, and children are armed.

The two camps march against each other. On the nights after the first two days of battle, the people rend the air with their cries of mourning and lamentation for the dead. Coriantumr tries to negotiate peace again, but the people are drunk with anger, fully in the power of Satan. In a little over a week, fighting each day, all the day long, sleeping on their swords by night, the armies slay all but a few of the strongest men on each side.

Finally, the end of the Jaredites comes, just as Ether had prophesied. Coriantumr cuts off the head of Shiz and becomes the sole survivor of his nation. Later, in further fulfillment of the prophecy, Coriantumr is found by the people of Zarahemla and dwells with them for nine months before he dies. (See Story 71.)

Gospel Principles:

1. **Anger.**
   - Anger quickly stole away any hope for peace. (See Ether 15:4-6.)
   - The warriors drank in anger until they became addicted and drunken with it. (See Ether 13:27; 15:22.)

2. **Blindness, Spiritual.** Coriantumr could not see what was happening to his people until things had become very extreme and out of his control. (See Ether 13:31; 15:1-3.)

3. **Choosing the right.** Coriantumr was plainly warned by the prophet, yet he chose not to repent. Therefore, he suffered the consequences of his choice. (See Ether 13:20-22; 15:33.)

4. **Grudge holding.** Shiz would not accept terms of peace. His oath to take revenge on Coriantumr overpowered his reason. (See Ether 14:24; 15:4-5 and 28-31.)

5. **Hardheartedness.** The hearts of the whole nation were so hardened that all the people refused to repent. (See Ether 13:17 and 22; 15:6.)

6. **Prophecy.** The prophecies of Ether were fulfilled, every whit. (See Ether 12:3; 13:20-22; 15:3 and 29-33; Omni 1:21.)

7. **Prophets.** The words of prophets are too often not believed until after they are fulfilled. (See Ether 13:22; 15:3.)

8. **Reward for wickedness.** The Jaredites paid an awful price for choosing wickedness over repentance, loss of: possessions, trust, peace, joy, and life itself. (See Ether 14:1-2, 8-10 and 25; 15:16-23.)

9. **Satan.** The destruction of the entire Jaredite nation was the quintessence of Satan's spiteful reign over men on the earth, his "finest" hour, filled with blood, hate, rage, and horror. What kind of life was it for these people? We get a glimpse of the awfulness of existing under the power of the Prince of Darkness. (See Ether 13:18-19, 25-26 and 31; 14:1-2, 8-10, 17-25, 27 and 31; 15:2 and 12-31, especially, Ether 15:19.)

10. **Stubbornness.** Two times Shiz refused offers of peace. He was unbending in his desire to kill Coriantumr. He was willing to lose all rather than repent. (See Ether 15:4-6, 18-19 and 28.)

11. **Trust in God.** Coriantumr trusted in his own wisdom, the cunning of the world, and rejected God's warning. Yet, in the end, it was only in fulfillment of prophecy that he survived. (See Ether 13:16-17 and 20-21; 14:24.)

12. **Vengeance.** Revenge is a vicious ping-pong ball that is batted back and forth. Unless one of the opponents is gracious enough to forgive and turn the other cheek, the end result is utter destruction. (See Ether 14:24-25; 15:6 and 28-29.)

* * *

STORY 80

MORONI FINISHES THE RECORD

Reference: Mormon 8:1-5 and 35-37; 9:30-34; Ether 1:1-2; 4:4-6; 5:1-6; 8:19-26; 12:22-29 and 36-41; Moroni 1:1-4; 10:1-7 and 27-34

Background: *Moroni was entrusted with the plates by his father, Mormon. These two men saw the great Nephite nation slaughtered down to twenty-four survivors. Then Moroni became the only Nephite left. He was caused to wander for over twenty years to protect his life. (See Story 70 and Mormon 8:1-14.)*

Story Outline: Moroni adds to his father's record. He writes to us as though we are present with him. He is concerned about the imperfections in the record, fearing that the Gentiles will mock because of his weakness in writing. Jesus appears to Moroni and comforts him, saying that the meek will not take advantage of his weakness.

Moroni gives us an account of the Jaredites, taken from the twenty-four gold plates, the Book of Ether. (See Stories 71 through 79.) As commanded by the Lord, he writes and seals up the things that the brother of Jared saw. (See Story 74.)

Moroni warns of the effects of secret combinations, realizing that the Jaredites and the Nephites were both brought down to destruction by these wicked organizations.

Prophetically, Moroni tells the future translator of the plates that there shall be three witnesses provided to establish the truth of the work of translation.

After completing the abridgement of Ether's record concerning the Jaredites, Moroni finds that he is still alive and writes some more things for our benefit. He gives a promise to those who will read the record that, through the power of the Holy Ghost, they may know of its truthfulness. He bids us farewell, exhorting us to come unto Christ that we may be made perfect in Him.

Gospel Principles:

1. **Church government.** The things that Moroni added to the record are of worth to us. In particular, it is of value to know how the Church was run in those times, the manner of ordination, baptism, sacrament, and discipline. (See Moroni 1:4. Also, see Moroni 2-6 and 8.)

2. **Courage.** Moroni refused to deny Christ, though it put his life in peril. (See Moroni 1:2-3.)

3. **Divine guidance.** Moroni added to the record the marvelous promise of divine revelation to the reader who is willing to ponder and pray sincerely. (See Moroni 10:1-6.)

4. **Enduring.** Moroni stayed true to the end of his life, all through his lonely wanderings as the sole survivor of a fallen nation. (See Mormon 8:3-5; Ether 12:38; Moroni 1:2-3; 10:34.)

5. **Jesus Christ.** One of the more valuable things Moroni added to his father's record was his testimony of the Savior. (See Ether 12:39-41.)

6. **Obedience.** Moroni followed the direction the Lord gave him to write and to seal up. (See Ether 4:5; 5:1.)

7. **Pearls before swine.** As a people, we have to repent if we want to be worthy of receiving more heavenly information. (See Ether 4:4-7.)

8. **Prophecy.** Prophecy spans the ages and connects the past and present with the future. Thus, Moroni was able to speak to us as though we were yet present with him. (See Mormon 8:35-37.)

9. **Resurrection.** What a firm conviction of the reality of the hereafter Moroni had! (See Ether 5:6; Moroni 10:34.)

10. **Steadfastness.** What a bleak sojourn in life was the lot of Moroni. He spent twenty years as a lone fugitive, yet still remained true to the end. (See Moroni 1:3.)

11. **Weakness.** What was perceived as weakness by Moroni, the Lord has turned into great strength. *The Book of Mormon* is a powerful book that "hisses forth" unto the convincing of men. (See Ether 12:23-29; Moroni 10:28-29.)

12. **Wisdom.** To learn from and avoid the mistakes of others is truly being wise. (See Mormon 9:31.)

13. **Witnesses.** Moroni gave instructions to the future translator of the plates that the truth of the book was to be established by the testimony of three witnesses. (See Ether 5:2-4.)

* * *

INDEX OF GOSPEL PRINCIPLES

Note: References in this index are to story numbers. For page numbers see the Table of Contents.

Humility, 3 Laman and Lemuel Murmur Against Their Father, 10 Nephi Breaks His Bow, 20 Ammon Returns to the Land of Nephi, 26 The Nephites Suffer in Bondage, 35 Alma Gives Up the Judgement-seat to Preach Repentance, 40 King Lamoni Is Converted Through Ammon's Efforts, 41 King Lamoni's Father Is Converted, 45 Alma Goes on a Mission to the Zoramites, 54 The Long War Is Brought to an End, 75 The Jaredites Cross the Sea to the Promised Land

Hypocrisy, 55 Prosperity Amongst the Nephites Leads to Pride and Defeat

Industry, 13 The Nephites Separate from the Lamanites, 21 Zeniff Goes Up to Possess the Land of Nephi, 53 Moroni Leaves the Battlefield to Re-establish the Government, 75 The Jaredites Cross the Sea to the Promised Land

Inspiration, see Divine guidance

Instruction, see Teaching

Integrity, 37 Zeezrom Is Caught in His Deceit and Repents, 46 Captain Moroni Stops the Lamanite Invasion by Stratagem

Jealousy, 13 The Nephites Separate from the Lamanites

Jesus Christ, 7 Lehi Has a Dream of the Tree and the Rod of Iron, 23 Abinadi Testifies Before King Noah, 30 Alma Establishes Churches in Zarahemla, 56 Nephi and Lehi Dedicate Themselves to Preaching the Word, 61 Samuel the Lamanite Prophesies to the Nephites, 62 The Signs of Christ's Birth Come to Pass, 65 The Resurrected Christ Appears to the People of Nephi, 67 Jesus Blesses the Nephite People, 74 The Brother of Jared Sees the Finger of the Lord, 77 The Jaredites Pass Through Cycles of Good and Evil, 80 Moroni Finishes the Record

Journals, 8 Nephi Keeps Two Sets of Plates, 15 Enos Prays All Day, 27 Limhi Discovers the 24 Gold Plates of the Jaredites, 68 Jesus Corrects the Records

Joy, also see Happiness, 5 Sariah Doubts and Complains, 7 Lehi Has a Dream of the Tree and the Rod of Iron, 19 King Benjamin Addresses His People, 39 Alma Has a Glad Reunion with the Sons of Mosiah, 67 Jesus Blesses the Nephite People, 69 The Effect of

* * *

INDEX OF PEOPLE, PLACES, THINGS, AND EVENTS

Note: References in this index are to story numbers. For page numbers see the Table of Contents.

Ammaron, record keeper, 69 The Effect of Christ's Visit Lasts Two Hundred Years, 70 Mormon and Moroni Witness the Final Destruction of the Nephites

Ammon, discoverer of Limhi's people in the land of Nephi, 20 Ammon Returns to the Land of Nephi, 21 Zeniff Goes Up to Possess the Land of Nephi, 27 Limhi Discovers the Twenty-four Gold Plates of the Jaredites, 28 Limhi's People Escape from Lamanite Bondage, 71 The History of the Jaredite Nation Is Revealed

Ammon, one of the four sons of Mosiah, 31 Alma the Younger and the Sons of Mosiah Are Converted, 39 Alma Has a Glad Reunion with the Sons of Mosiah, 40 King Lamoni Is Converted Through Ammon's Efforts, 41 King Lamoni's Father Is Converted, 42 Aaron Preaches to the Lamanites, 43 The Anti-Nephi-Lehies Bury Their Swords

Ammon, People of, 43 The Anti-Nephi-Lehies Bury Their Swords, 44 Korihor Is Struck Dumb, 45 Alma Goes on a Mission to the Zoramites, 46 Captain Moroni Stops the Lamanite Invasion by Stratagem, 51 Helaman's Two Thousand Stripling Warriors Are Preserved by Faith

Ammonihah, City of, land of, 36 Alma and Amulek Preach in Ammonihah, 37 Zeezrom Is Caught in His Deceit and Repents, 38 The City of Ammonihah Is Destroyed by the Lamanites, 43 The Anti-Nephi-Lehies Bury Their Swords, 48 Amalickiah Becomes King by Treachery

Ammoron, Lamanite king, 50 Nephite King-men Weaken Their Nation's Defense, 54 The Long War Is Brought to an End

Amnigaddah, Jaredite king, 77 The Jaredites Pass Through Cycles of Good and Evil

Amulek, missionary companion of Alma, 36 Alma and Amulek Preach in Ammonihah, 37 Zeezrom Is Caught in His Deceit and Repents, 38 The City of Ammonihah Is Destroyed by the Lamanites, 45 Alma Goes on a Mission to the Zoramites

Amulon, Land of, 29 Alma and His Followers Sojourn in the Wilderness

Amulon, priest of Noah, 29 Alma and His Followers Sojourn in the Wilderness

Addresses His People, 23 Abinadi Testifies Before King Noah, 25 Wicked King Noah Is Put to Death, 26 The Nephites Suffer in Bondage, 34 Amlici Seeks to Be King, 36 Alma and Amulek Preach in Ammonihah, 38 The City of Ammonihah Is Destroyed by the Lamanites 61 Samuel the Lamanite Prophesies to the Nephites, 62 The Signs of Christ's Birth Come to Pass, 65 The Resurrected Christ Appears to the People of Nephi, 68 Jesus Corrects the Records, 72 Jared and His Family Are Not Confounded, 78 The Prophet Ether Witnesses the Destruction of the Jaredites, 79 Coriantumr Chooses Destruction over Repentance, 80 Moroni Finishes the Record

Prophets, 1 Lehi Preaches in Jerusalem, 14 Sherem Denies Christ, 20 Ammon Returns to the Land of Nephi, 22 King Noah Turns His Kingdom to Wickedness, 23 Abinadi Testifies Before King Noah, 24 Alma Organizes the Church in the Wilderness, 46 Captain Moroni Stops the Lamanite Invasion by Stratagem, 58 Nephi Reveals the Murder of the Chief Judge, 59 Nephi Asks for a Famine to Humble the Nephites, 61 Samuel the Lamanite Prophesies to the Nephites, 62 The Signs of Christ's Birth Come to Pass, 64 The Nephite Government Is Broken Up, 65 The Resurrected Christ Appears to the People of Nephi, 68 Jesus Corrects the Records, 76 Jaredite Kings Vie for Power, 77 The Jaredites Pass Through Cycles of Good and Evil, 78 The Prophet Ether Witnesses the Destruction of the Jaredites, 79 Coriantumr Chooses Destruction over Repentance

Prosperity, 33 The Church Endures Trials under the Reign of the Judges, 55 Prosperity Amongst the Nephites Leads to Pride and Defeat, 59 Nephi Asks for a Famine to Humble the Nephites, 60 The Nephites Turn Away from God Again

Provisions, 2 Lehi Takes His Family into the Wilderness, 12 Lehi's Family Crosses the Ocean, 28 Limhi's People Escape from Lamanite Bondage, 51 Helaman's Two Thousand Stripling Warriors Are Preserved by Faith, 72 Jared and His Family Are Not Confounded, 73 The Brother of Jared Forgets to Pray, 75 The Jaredites Cross the Sea to the Promised Land

Queens, 40 King Lamoni Is Converted Through Ammon's Efforts, 41 King Lamoni's Father Is Converted, 48 Amalickiah Becomes King by Treachery

Forgets to Pray, 75 The Jaredites Cross the Sea to the Promised Land

Seashores, 11 Nephi Builds a Ship, 50 Nephite King-men Weaken Their Nation's Defense, 73 The Brother of Jared Forgets to Pray

Secret combinations, 57 Nephite Peace Is Destroyed by the Gadianton Robbers, 64 The Nephite Government Is Broken Up, 69 The Effect of Christ's Visit Lasts Two Hundred Years, 77 The Jaredites Pass Through Cycles of Good and Evil, 78 The Prophet Ether Witnesses the Destruction of the Jaredites, 79 Coriantumr Chooses Destruction over Repentance, 80 Moroni Finishes the Record

Seeds, 12 Lehi's Family Crosses the Ocean, 21 Zeniff Goes Up to Possess the Land of Nephi, 45 Alma Goes on a Mission to the Zoramites, 73 The Brother of Jared Forgets to Pray

Serpents, 77 The Jaredites Pass Through Cycles of Good and Evil

Servants, 4 Lehi's Sons Obtain the Brass Plates, 40 King Lamoni Is Converted Through Ammon's Efforts, 41 King Lamoni's Father Is Converted, 49 The People of Morianton Rebel over a Land Claim

Shared, Jaredite king, 79 Coriantumr Chooses Destruction over Repentance

Sheep, 30 Alma Establishes Churches in Zarahemla

Shelem, Mount, 74 The Brother of Jared Sees the Finger of the Lord

Sherem, 14 Sherem Denies Christ

Shez, Jaredite king, 77 The Jaredites Pass Through Cycles of Good and Evil

Shiblon, Jaredite king, 77 The Jaredites Pass Through Cycles of Good and Evil

Shilom, Land of, 20 Ammon Returns to the Land of Nephi, 21 Zeniff Goes Up to Possess the Land of Nephi

Ships, 9 A Compass (Liahona) Guides Lehi's Family, 11 Nephi Builds a Ship, 12 Lehi's Family Crosses the Ocean

Shiz, Jaredite leader, 78 The Prophet Ether Witnesses the Destruction of the Jaredites

Shule, Jaredite king, 76 Jaredite Kings Vie for Power

Sidom, Land of, 37 Zeezrom Is Caught in His Deceit and Repents

Treaties, 70 Mormon and Moroni Witness the Final Destruction of the Nephites, 79 Coriantumr Chooses Destruction over Repentance

Trees, 7 Lehi Has a Dream of the Tree and the Rod of Iron

Trembling, 37 Zeezrom Is Caught in His Deceit and Repents

Tribes, 64 The Nephite Government Is Broken Up

Valleys, 3 Laman and Lemuel Murmur Against Their Father, 8 Nephi Keeps Two Sets of Plates, 9 A Compass (Liahona) Guides Lehi's Family, 29 Alma and His Followers Sojourn in the Wilderness

Visions, 1 Lehi Preaches in Jerusalem, 7 Lehi Has a Dream of the Tree and the Rod of Iron, 40 King Lamoni Is Converted Through Ammon's Efforts

Voice of the people, 34 Amlici Seeks to Be King

Voices, 30 Alma Establishes Churches in Zarahemla, 31 Alma the Younger and the Sons of Mosiah Are Converted, 56 Nephi and Lehi Dedicate Themselves to Preaching the Word, 62 The Signs of Christ's Birth Come to Pass, 65 The Resurrected Christ Appears to the People of Nephi

Walls, 20 Ammon Returns to the Land of Nephi, 36 Alma and Amulek Preach in Ammonihah, 50 Nephite King-men Weaken Their Nation's Defense, 54 The Long War Is Brought to an End, 56 Nephi and Lehi Dedicate Themselves to Preaching the Word, 61 Samuel the Lamanite Prophesies to the Nephites

Warnings, 10 Nephi Breaks His Bow, 13 The Nephites Separate from the Lamanites, 15 Enos Prays All Day, 16 Mosiah Discovers Zarahemla and the Mulekites, 23 Abinadi Testifies Before King Noah, 24 Alma Organizes the Church in the Wilderness, 27 Limhi Discovers the Twenty-four Gold Plates of the Jaredites, 36 Alma and Amulek Preach in Ammonihah, 61 Samuel the Lamanite Prophesies to the Nephites

Wars, 8 Nephi Keeps Two Sets of Plates, 16 Mosiah Discovers Zarahemla and the Mulekites, 21 Zeniff Goes Up to Possess the Land of Nephi, 48 Amalickiah Becomes King by Treachery, 54 The Long War Is Brought to an End, 59 Nephi Asks for a Famine to Humble the Nephites, 76 Jaredite Kings Vie for Power, 77 The Jaredites Pass Through Cycles of Good and Evil, 78 The Prophet

* * *

Printed in the United States
By Bookmasters